Ragnar's Guide to
Interviews,
Investigations
Interrogations
and

Ragnar's Guide to

Interviews, Investigations and Interrogations

How to Conduct Them, How to Survive Them

Ragnar Benson

Paladin Press • Boulder, Colorado

Also by Ragnar Benson:
Acquiring New ID
Bull's-Eye: Crossbows
Do-It-Yourself Medicine
Eating Cheap
Hardcore Poaching
Live Off the Land in the City and Country
Mantrapping
Modern Survival Retreat
Modern Weapons Caching
Ragnar's Action Encyclopedias, Volumes 1 and 2
Ragnar's Guide to the Underground Economy
Ragnar's Ten Best Traps . . . And a Few Others That Are Damn Good, Too
Ragnar's Urban Survival
Survival Nursing
Survival Poaching
Survivalist's Medicine Chest
The Survival Retreat: A Total Plan for Retreat Defense
Switchblade: The Ace of Blades

*Ragnar's Guide to Interviews, Investigations, and Interrogations:
How to Conduct Them, How to Survive Them*
by Ragnar Benson

Copyright © 2000 by Ragnar Benson
ISBN 1-58160-095-X
Printed in the United States of America

Published by Paladin Press, a division of
Paladin Enterprises, Inc.
Gunbarrel Tech Center
7077 Winchester Circle
Boulder, Colorado 80306, USA
+ 1.303.443.7250

Direct inquiries and/or orders to the above address.

Visit our Web site at www.paladin-press.com

CONTENTS

PREFACE

Is there any question in the reader's mind that we live in an extremely litigious society? Lawyers and judges for whom I often work tell me there is a virtual 100-percent certainty that all of us will eventually, at some time during our three-score-and-ten journey of travail and tears, end up as a defendant, plaintiff, or witness in some sort of legal proceeding.

Acting as a participant in legal proceedings is frequently done on an involuntary basis and may include the following:

- Routine interviews by investigatory—private or civil (police)—personnel that go no further than securing your personal opinion about what you saw, heard, smelled, or tasted in a specific circumstance currently of interest to the law, the courts, or both. Frequently, these interviews are concluded rapidly after the investigator discovers that what you saw, heard, touched, or smelled had little or no bearing on the matter at hand.

- Official, court-ordered subpoenas requiring your appearance in court or at an attorney's office to provide sworn testimony relative to legal proceedings. These proceedings can be either criminal or civil. A summons usually signals the start of what could be protracted legal proceedings.

- Sworn testimony, known as depositions. Depositions have become frightfully common, in lockstep with our society's litigation explosion. The threat of a time-consuming, often humiliating, frightening deposition is a common tool of the investigator. You may be deposed when the opposite side of a legal struggle wants to hear your interpretation of what you saw or heard or to evaluate your knowledge, expertise, and standing relative to the case. Depositions are done under oath in front of a court reporter and, as mentioned, are often used as a threat by investigators to get you to talk informally about the issue at hand.

- Voluntary or mandatory requests to act as a material witness. You can become a material witness suddenly and capriciously. For instance, a nurse standing on a corner at 3:00 A.M. after her shift at the hospital witnesses a car that was standing at a stop sign be crunched by a pickup truck full of drunk females going what she estimates to be 40 miles over the speed limit. She is the only witness. Her testimony may be biased against drunks, pickup trucks, or single women driving around alone at 3:00 A.M., but it is all investigators have, other than expert or (more commonly) scientific evidence (e.g., skid marks, blood alcohol levels, damage to the vehicles).

- Opportunities to act as an expert witness pursuant to legal proceedings. Before personally ruling out this category, I often recall the answer given by my high school composition teacher when asked why she arbitrarily assigned term paper subjects. "Every kid in this school," she said, "is an expert on something I know nothing about. And I don't want to be led down the primrose path into a subject about which I cannot determine whether the writer is blowing smoke!" All of us are probably expert in some area, no matter how trivial.

Able, high-powered attorneys and their investigators often call three or four experts in any given area of litigation. They do this to learn how to talk to opposing experts. This may include matters as mundane as the custom of the trade when cutting hair, tailoring a woman's dress, laying waste-water pipe, unplugging a sewer, frying hamburgers, or selling antiques. Part of an investigator's job involves locating articulate, presentable experts who can do a good job of educating the attorney and who are credible in court.

- Criminal interrogations relative to crimes you may or may not have committed. This category may be included in others previously mentioned. In our modern American society, anyone can be accused of some kind of crime any time officials wish to do so. Wise citizens do not rule out being arbitrarily charged with some sort of civil or criminal breach. Offenses with which you may be accused may be as trivial as speeding or as heinous as statutory rape. More than any other category, speeding includes many opportunities for game playing. For instance, cops often practice their interrogation skills on speeders, and all of us get speeding tickets from time to time.

- Prisoner of war or hostage-type situations. Admittedly these are not a common concern for most of us, but techniques used under these circumstances will be "the same only different" from other categories. Military interrogation is an interesting business, and readers may as well know the basic rules of the road.

None of us knows what the future will bring. Readers may be interested in the process of interrogation because they wish to become private investigators or because they are already private investigators and want to refine and improve their skills. Or they may simply be private individuals who wish to avoid investigations intelligently and effectively or to neutralize legal proceedings.

Can skilled, informed readers learn to survive skilled investigators? I can only answer from my point of view. Given my 26 years of experience as an investigator, could I personally contend with a really skilled investigator? Guaranteed, the answer will surprise and perhaps anger some readers!

The best way to teach a potential witness how to survive interviews or interrogations is to show how they are done. So that's the perspective of this book. Using actual case studies as examples, I show how the best investigators and attorneys in the business interview witnesses—how they get them talking and keep them talking until they get all the information they can from them. Of course, if you're the potential witness, the best thing for you is to know how an interviewer thinks and the tricks he will use to get you to blab all. So you just consider everything in this book from a defensive perspective. At the end of certain chapters you'll see tips that give specific advice to witnesses on how to avoid or manage an interview or interrogation.

INTRODUCTION

As an experienced private investigator, I am often asked to list fatal flaws frequently observed in private investigation techniques. Three come immediately to mind:

- *Not working hard enough.* Investigators, both public and private, simply do not work hard enough to turn over every rock and pebble and pursue every lead no matter how thin.
- *Not listening.* The super salesmen do well enough on pretexts but cannot bring themselves to shut up and listen thoughtfully to what the witness has to say, as well as observe his body language. Many investigators, including cops, are desperately trying to formulate their next question so as not to look stupid instead. In our culture, listening is really difficult—especially when we suspect we

already know the answer, we realize it's mostly smoke the witness is generating, or the witness is obviously trying to manipulate us. I overcome my tendency not to listen by putting down *only* direct quotes from witnesses in my reports. It got embarrassing and time consuming to have to go back to witnesses to get enough quotes for a proper report. This makes me listen closely the first time.

- *Not knowing what is important and not knowing when to stop.* Otherwise competent and energetic investigators often gather tremendous amounts of information of absolutely no value to the case at hand. It probably does no good, for instance, for an investigator to find out that an accused computer hacker likes bananas and cornflakes for lunch or that his sister drives a Ford. You gotta learn what is important. Likewise you gotta know when to stop investigating someone. It is true that good investigators must kiss a great many toads to find a prince, but they must also learn to recognize a prince when they have one.

As with all of life, the devil is in the details. What seems simple enough in concept is not nearly so simple when it comes time for real-life implementation. We'll see this proven true over and over in the following chapters as I address how private investigators, cops, attorneys, and military interrogators *really* conduct interviews, investigations, and interrogations.

WHAT MAKES A SUCCESSFUL INVESTIGATOR?

THERE ARE ALL KINDS OF INVESTIGATORS OUT THERE, and each has his own way of conducting investigations. But there are several rules that successful investigators seem to follow. In this chapter we are going to discuss the most important of these.

HARD WORK PAYS OFF

It's amazing how lucky you can be when you work very, very hard. If one compelling, overriding, guiding, infallible rule characterizes the business of doing investigations, it is the above. This rule applies to private as well as police investigators. Wise folks falling on either side of the issue will note it carefully.

Often police-type investigators will be severely limited by the amount of time they can put into a case. "So many criminals and so few hours in the day" seems to be their plaintive cry.

Commonly, private investigators are hired because they have the time and energy to devote to a specific situation. Of course, private investigators are frequently limited by the financial resources of their clients. All of us have come very close to resolving some particularly dicey situations only to have our clients tell us, "Sorry, we are absolutely out of money."

I recently worked for the defense on a case where a young woman was charged with statutory rape. We had everything going nicely in our favor when she told us that she was going to have to pull the cork financially. Fortunately, the prosecutor didn't know this. All he saw was our very determined, thorough preparation to that point, and that scared him off. He threw in the towel just hours before trial time, not knowing that we were very close to doing the same thing.

FOLLOW EVERY LEAD

It's the duty of an investigator to come up with that one piece of evidence that no one knew was out there, upon which the entire case can be made to turn. Often it does not exist, but good investigators are characterized by their great optimism that it's out there waiting to be found. Second only to the rule about luck following hard work, investigators believe this one most: *Those who venture nothing will have nothing.*

How to find this evidence when no one even knows it exists? The answer is that good investigators work very hard to turn over absolutely every rock, pebble, and board, and to pursue absolutely every lead to its final, often bitter, end. This requires a bright, listening, observant, alert, self-starting investigator sensitive to hints or leads that others—because of lack of experience or laziness—may ignore.

I recently worked a murder case for the defendant. There was no question that the defendant had stabbed the deceased, but was the crime premeditated? If so, did the county really want to go to the added expense of a "murder-one" (first-degree murder) trial, or would it be better to go for murder two, where premeditation did not have to be proved? The prosecutor was leaning toward murder two, but our client wanted to plead spousal abuse. Of course, in our liberal society, many self-proclaimed experts were willing to step forward to support that defense. The defendant's attorney—my employer in this case—said it would be a disaster to pursue that defense in a county composed of farmers, miners, loggers, and ranchers, who would sit on her jury, because they would not sympathize with that defense. He was dead right on that one.

During my first two weeks on the case I interviewed literally scores of potential witnesses. Although the incident occurred deep in the forest, far from any dwellings, I did manage to scare up a camper who was an "ear-witness" to the incident. But a nagging hunch remained, suggesting that someone was still out there who knew more about what had happened. Actually it was more than a hunch—numerous witnesses with whom I had talked referred to a mysterious, so far invisible, boyfriend.

One day, my office phone rang, and the caller identified himself as someone with information about the case.

"Hi," an unfamiliar voice said, "it's Bruce _____. I am sitting down at the Longline Café drinking coffee. I am the fellow you have been looking for the last month. I am tired of hiding."

I was pleased that he was tired of hiding, even though I didn't know that is what he had been doing—and it had been two weeks, not a month, that I had been looking for him. And I was also pleased he had called me. Usually I have to call witnesses—few potential witnesses actually call me.

"If you come right down," Bruce said, "we can have coffee, and I will tell you what I know about the murder."

It was from this fellow that I learned for certain that a week before murdering her husband in an alleged drunken brawl my client had told Bruce (who was, of course, the mysterious boyfriend) that she was going to kill her husband and run off with Bruce to live happily ever after. If the prosecuting attorney found out about my client's boyfriend, we now had a murder-one defense on our hands, but that isn't the real point in this instance.

As it relates to this book, it is important to understand that this fellow voluntarily came in to talk because he perceived that a very thorough, meticulous investigation was in progress, which would eventually sweep him into the system no matter how much he tried to avoid it. That winter was coming on and he was tired of living alone in a cold tent in the mountains also helped immeasurably. Investigators take whatever fortuitous circumstances come their way with thanks.

In this case it was the prosecuting attorney who was lazy. He never did find out about Bruce. As far as I know, he never even suspected there was a witness such as Bruce out there.

KNOW THE LEGAL THEORIES

The murder case discussed above turned on premeditation that, in this circumstance, was simple legal logic. This brings up the third vital rule of witness interrogation, evidence gathering, and all legal investigations in general: *Know beyond a shadow of doubt what legal theory or theories drive specific cases.*

Some investigators do not discover these theories until after they have interviewed three or four witnesses. Some, to their credit, sit down with the lead attorney at the beginning to know exactly what theories are being pursued in a specific case. Often just reading briefs, complaints, depositions, and interrogatories for a new case will take the first couple of days.

Wise investigators usually do not talk to key witnesses until they understand the case thoroughly. Taking the defendant's word for what is and is not important to the case is usually a non-starter. Defendants, even if they are attorneys, often have weird, sometimes irrational theories about their situations that may lead unwary investigators into a legal cul-de-sac. It's okay to placate a client a bit by interviewing Aunt Emma about voices in the garage or pursuing rumors of dirty pictures involving the local police chief, but only if the client has unusually deep pockets.

On the other hand, attorneys frequently send me out to talk to their clients, just to give the impression that something is being done about their case. Doing this type of public relations for the attorney is necessary, but the situation can get dicey for inexperienced investigators who don't understand their real role in these circumstances.

GOOD INVESTIGATORS MUST BE GOOD SALESMEN

Universally, judges, attorneys, investigators, and many cops agree that good investigators must be outstanding salesmen, with huge amounts of successful sales experience behind them. This sales experience does *not* include standing next to a cash register at Wal-Mart, ringing up purchases. It must be something real like selling cars, encyclopedias, life insurance, Bibles, appliances, or investment plans, or it could be fund-raising. In my case I believe my best boost came from working with a tycoon billionaire who loved to raise money for causes. He was one of the best salesmen around when it came to talking people into giving money. "You gotta give them a good reason to give you their money," he often told me.

Good investigators always come from a sales background. The cop or investigator who interviews you might well moonlight at "Friendly Bob's Used Car Sales."

Another example of a super-salesman is John Banderson of Boise, Idaho. John isn't an investigator, but he is without question the best salesman who ever walked the face of the earth. I include this example here so you can see how a real salesman works and what you as an investigator can learn from him.

Against insurmountable odds, Banderson thought of the one reason in the whole world I should purchase his 40-foot motor home. Under normal circumstances I am a happy but modest tent-and-campfire kind of guy. Even thinking of purchasing an $80,000 rolling place to sleep is rank idiocy in my opinion. But John knew what it would take to sell me on the idea of buying his motor home when normally I wouldn't even consider such insanity.

"You can keep all of your hunting, fishing, and camping gear, plus your hunting clothes, in one place in the mobile home," he explained. "When you return home after a very busy day, you can immediately, without thinking, jump into this machine and take off on what you know will be a successful hunting or fishing trip. You know the trip will be successful because you will have all your gear. The price of my motor home is modest compared to the hundreds of successful hunting and fishing trips you will take with it," Banderson finished with a flourish.

It was the only reason for ownership that made any sense to me at all. If it hadn't been for an alert wife's pointing out that I didn't have $80,000 to spend on a tin teepee and that she would gladly see that gun, ammo, boots, jacket, and gloves were always waiting in a bag in the garage, I might have actually bought the silly thing. Just thinking about the closeness of it all gives me the willies.

That's how good these sales pros are, and that's why the chapter on pretexts (page 29) is so important. Just like you've got to give people a good reason for them to give you their money, you've also got to give them a good reason to tell you the stuff you want to know, and that's what pretexts are all about.

Debate swirls around the question of whether ex-cops of one kind or another or ex-salesmen of broad experience make the most effective private investigators. Conditions are changing among more intelligent, dedicated members of the law enforcement community, but many experts who have seen it both ways do not care for the often blunt, unfriendly, unimaginative investigative conduct of ex-cops. Cops tend to rely on the authority of the uniform, badge, and gun (not necessarily in that order) to get what they want, rather than their salesmanship.

Actually, the best cops for investigative/interrogation work are those who have also moonlighted as used-car salesmen. But, of course, the general public and the cops' co-workers would react in horror to that suggestion.

In addition, most investigators with a law enforcement background tend to rely on computer data banks, large amounts of backup staff, and lab analysis when common sense, salesmanship, and practical knowledge might be better. There is also the bureaucratic lack of initiative that works against people with public agency backgrounds. Many simply do not have the ambition and optimism necessary to get the job started, much less completed.

GET THE WITNESS TO TALK AND
KEEP THE INTERVIEW GOING

Another basic investigator's guideline comes straight out of military interrogation: *Never fail to learn something about the case from every witness, as long as that witness will talk even briefly.*

How to keep a witness talking? Besides having a glib mouth and being the rare listener in our society, the answer is so simple, yet I still have to write it down on my interview pad from time to time. In short, almost choppy segments, I want to have detailed answers to the five Ws—who, what, where, when, and why. Conversation in these areas should never lag unless the investigator has such ego problems that he simply cannot listen and ask questions. (More on the art and science of listening and observing in Chapter 2.)

Literally thousands of subsets exist to the five Ws: How old is the subject? What did she look like? How did she dress? How was her grooming? Did she talk like an educated person? Did you see anything that looked like shoplifted goods? How well do you recall this incident? As you get into a case, added bits of information can be thrown in to "refresh" the witnesses' memory. But be careful: your job is to find out what the subjects know, not lead them into believing what you know.

Before getting into the meat of the subject, good investigators will attempt to build rapport with witnesses by appearing concerned and friendly, listening, and talking just enough to keep things moving while looking for subtle indications about how that person personally feels about the case. If possible, talk to witnesses about the weather, their hobbies, their employment backgrounds, their past experiences with our legal system, their cars, or their grandkids (in the case of older people). In this regard, women seem better at small talk than men.

Knowing when to taper your questions and comments and allow the witnesses to "talk their guts out" is extremely important. Many especially glib investigators have large egos and cannot shut up and let the other guy explain what he saw. Expert investigators claim that the really good stuff comes rushing out in a torrent the last five minutes of the interview, when the witness thinks the investigator is through and lets down his guard.

Even experienced witnesses find it difficult not to talk too much in front of experienced investigators. I believe that it's virtually impossible not to talk too much in front of an experienced investigator with a well-thought-through plan.

Be extremely alert to uncovering the existence of other corroborating witnesses, documents, news stories, or anything else while conducting an interview. Jump on anything that is said that might have a bearing on the case.

Examples abound. A store owner in a tiny farming community casually mentioned during an interview that a woman I was investigating for a wrongful injury suit had been accused of murdering her newborn baby many years before. When I brought in the newspaper story about the incident, the case against my client suddenly evaporated. This doesn't make complete sense legally, but it's what happened.

In another instance, my client was severely injured by his estranged son-in-law during the course of a foolish argument between two older adults. Just by chance, while interviewing some people in the community about the incident, I discovered that the son-in-law was a high school wrestling champion and had briefly worked as a wrestling coach many years ago. On learning of our discovery, he (and probably his insurance company) quickly came up with a high-five-figure cash settlement offer. This case was one of those strange instances of a combination civil/legal affair that one encounters only a few times in a lifetime.

Keeping a witness talking is especially tough when he keeps saying, "I don't know." The next time try breaking the "I don't know" down into small parts. "*What* don't you know—the color of the car, the license number, what street it was on, the identity of the driver, whether the passengers were drinking, or whether the driver of the other vehicle was actually dead?" Often this little ploy gets witnesses rattling on a mile a minute.

WHAT ABOUT BRIBERY?

Do investigators use bribery to gather information? Yes—but very carefully. In some cases, such as securing specific bank and phone records, it may be the only game in town. Yet, bribery can be like torture in reverse. Careless investigators can keep passing out cash until the person receiving the largess can no longer think of reasons for them to do so or they run out of cash. If this isn't a pretext on the part of the witness, I don't know what is. But both the witness and the investigator know it is the only way information will pass.

For example, it is common for investigators to pay $50 to each neighbor who agrees to call when an elusive key witness stops by his house. In another instance, a jilted wife or girlfriend may appreciate cash in payment for information about her "ex" or his parents. These folks have a very finely tuned sense of how much cash they can wring out of investigators.

Somewhat like physical torture is for military interrogation (as you'll see in Chapter 8), pay for information is the blunt instrument of the private investigation trade. But it should be specific pay for specific, measurable performance. Investigators must be certain they get usable information for their clients' cash, or the expense won't be allowed in their expense account.

DON'T INTIMIDATE WITNESSES BY TAKING NOTES

Do investigators write down comments as they go? Some witnesses become anxious to very anxious about yellow pads. I am prepared to go either way. Often I will ask if the witness will feel threatened if I take notes. "I like to take down your exact comments as we go along," I often say, "because I am not smart enough to remember all of this." Acting so dumb that the witness is made to feel in control is often helpful. Some witnesses are sufficiently flattered that they dominate the conversation to my advantage. If during the interview I cannot take notes, after the interview I drive down the street 500 yards and immediately pull over to jot everything down while it's still fresh in my mind.

One thing is certain, if it's a tough, acrimonious case involving recalcitrant, hardened witnesses, don't carry a notepad that has anything written on it into the interview. I learned this the hard way a few years back when a tough, old parolee roughly grabbed my pad and started reading statements made by other witnesses. Use an empty notepad whenever dealing with experienced people!

RESEARCH THE BACKGROUNDS OF SUBJECTS

There is another syndrome of our current society that applies to investigators. Jurors, attorneys, and some judges tend to evaluate a witness not on whether that witness' observations are true or false, logical or illogical, but rather on the basis of who is doing the saying. For instance, I have had shrewd attorneys cast doubt upon witnesses I found by emphasizing that these people tended to vote Republican, were environmentalists, or were of a particular ethnic background. This kind of strategy can occasionally be turned to your client's advantage, but be aware that in our culture people (including jury members) may throw out truth that has been corroborated by as many as three different witnesses because they personally dislike the message bearer. For example, a woman recently told me I shouldn't believe anything in a certain book because Dan Quayle was on the publisher's board of directors! Nothing in this business should surprise us any more.

GOOD INVESTIGATORS MUST BE GOOD ACTORS

Like top trial lawyers, good investigators must be good actors. No unrehearsed reversal or sudden revelation should visibly surprise them, unless done for theatrical effect. Effective investigators always maintain a stone face and a fallback question on the tip of their tongues with which to mask sudden surprise while regrouping their thoughts.

On the other hand, experts recommend that if, by some fortuitous circumstance, a witness unexpectedly drops a stunning piece of favorable information, you slide right past it without obvious emotion while evaluating what you just received. Later, after considering its implications, you may come back to this issue for amplification and clarification. This is another one of those simple rules that is the devil to implement correctly when it actually comes up!

I recently had the occasion to practice my acting ability when I caught a cop in an absolutely overt, obvious, obnoxious, stunning lie right in front of fellow officers. The other officers should have hidden their reactions better, but their obvious surprise at his lie gave the hapless fellow away. However, I slid right on past like nothing had happened, allowing everyone to save some face. But for a moment you could have cut the embarrassment in the room with a knife.

LIES CAN BE USEFUL IN GETTING AT THE TRUTH

Scaring witnesses with a vague hint at some "hidden" evidence is a common tactic on both sides of criminal cases and in some civil cases. Cops often tell suspects that someone on the street saw them and turned in a perfect description, that they have the suspect's fingerprints from the crime scene, or that a buddy just confessed. A cop once told my wife that he had plaster casts of my jeep tracks. She knew that the incident he was investigating didn't involve our jeep and the cop was lying. This was her first experience with police investigators, and she has not viewed things the same since that incident.

This tactic also works for private investigators. I have personally demolished many civil and criminal cases by alluding to some sort of phony evidence. A recent statutory rape case provides a good example.

During my questioning of the alleged victim's mother, I alluded to some strange, very private markings on the defendant that the alleged victim could not have failed to notice given her graphic account of the sexual encounter. No such marks existed on the accused, but word that they did got back to the alleged victim through her mother. The vague hint was that when the daughter could not say that she saw these peculiar marks during her encounter, the accused would prove in court that they did exist, destroying the alleged account of what happened. The girl and her mother both left the state one night without pursuing the case.

Almost all investigators use these types of devices to scare off people and discourage them from making phony allegations.

USE THE CALL OF CELEBRITY TO IMPRESS WITNESSES

Investigators sometimes play on the fact that some witnesses enjoy their momentary notoriety. "You are an important person with something valuable to offer," the investigator implies subtly. The only times this fails completely are (1) when the witnesses have already been repeatedly and rudely dragged through the system and know they will be dropped like a dead skunk when they are no longer needed and (2) when investigators tip their hand about who they are really supporting with the investigation.

THERE IS NO HONOR AMONG THIEVES

The idea of honor among thieves is a complete myth. Cops know this, often playing one thief against another to get confessions, and so do good investigators. In one notable instance, a man whose close buddy was sent to the joint for life could have helped his friend but wouldn't so much as talk to me—principally, I believe, because he was running around with the wife of the guy in the slammer and wanted his "friend" to remain put away. Sometimes this is a very crummy business.

USE HUMOR TO PUT WITNESSES AT EASE

Investigators should take a lesson from good trial lawyers and learn to employ wit to relax and win over the people they are questioning. For example, Wyoming defense attorney Gerry Spence is noted for his mastery of humor and self-evasive wit in front of juries. Spence's down-home attitude often wins over juries when facts and logic get confused. Like trial lawyers, investigators must learn to be excellent "song-and-dance" performers in order to get the most out of their subjects.

KNOW HOW TO USE CAMERAS AND ELECTRONIC EQUIPMENT

Interviews are the heart of the investigator's profession, but there is more to it than just talking to people and gathering information. Using cameras to document evidence is a good example.

Private investigators must be very good with cameras under what are often extremely stressful, difficult circumstances. Opportunities in this business seldom repeat themselves. Excuses such as "My camera wasn't working" or "I used the wrong settings" won't cut it. Keeping in practice requires shooting at least a roll of film a week in each camera. Most investigators use two or even three cameras with a half-dozen or more universally interchangeable lenses.

All investigators use video cameras because of the nature of the work they do. A good supply of extra batteries, rechargers, and tapes is also required. Although many courts will not allow video evidence, investigators still gather it to use as background on the case.

I don't do wiretaps or bug sweeps myself. This is a very specialized business, and it is simply too time consuming and expensive for most investigators to stay properly current. Instead I have an electronics expert who often "joint-ventures" with me when needed.

STICK TO THE FACTS WHEN WRITING REPORTS

Good investigators are aware that long, inane written reports wear attorneys down, needlessly run up clients' bills, and may destroy the investigators' credibility. Investigators should list only the names of people contacted in pursuit of certain facts when doing their write-ups, *not* a bunch of miscellaneous details about these folks' not knowing anything.

DON'T MAKE TROUBLE FOR YOURSELF

Let the record note that, except in one notable instance on a murder case, I have never dealt with a partially clothed, beautiful young woman. It happens so infrequently that it would be foolish to go into this business expecting such. As a matter of policy, if I suspect a female witness is young, handsome (as we more charitably refer to them in the trade), and pertinent to an investigation, I only interview her in a public place. This leads to lots of interrogations on front steps or sidewalks. It's my job to keep sight of the fact that I am trying to get a person out of trouble, not create new trouble.

What about firearms? Several attorneys and judges I know who employ private investigators are adamant that they will not hire any investigator who carries a gun. This weeds out those who go into the business because they want to "carry." Sorry about this, those of you who watch lots of television. Experts who frequently use investigative services validly ask, "Whom are you going to shoot with your pistol—a witness?" Most feel they have enough trouble on any given case without having to deal with some sort of silly weapons allegations.

THERE ARE NO GUARANTEES . . .

Even if an investigator does everything he's supposed to do, there is no guarantee about what will happen.

In one case, I labored mightily to prove that the alleged victim of a rape was so drunk she could not have known what was going on. Since absolutely no physical evidence existed, it was her word against my client's. I determined that the alleged victim had consumed two and a half 40-ounce bottles of Old

English beer containing 7.5 percent alcohol in less than 90 minutes, prior to the alleged incident. Under questioning, she finally admitted to this. It was a rate of consumption that experts were willing to testify would have rendered her near comatose, especially at her young age! With this disclosure, we probably had the case won, but my client was emotionally unable to pursue the matter. In court he plea-bargained for a lesser offense and sentence rather than going to trial. Here, my client spent a great deal of money for something he ultimately didn't use.

People who go into the investigation business so they can carry guns or meet beautiful women will likely be disappointed.

I have investigated a number of relatively high-profile criminal cases. Of these, I can recall only one in which what really happened, including the details, was not uncovered. And there was only one case where (in my opinion) justice was not served. In this instance (again, in my opinion), justice was dramatically overdone. The client got 18 years for what was essentially a first offense—there wasn't even a parking ticket in his background.

It is not my goal to personally pass judgment on the guilt or innocence of my clients, but rather to obtain the greatest amount of justice along with offering reasonable and prudent compassion. People in our culture can be very critical of that philosophy. "The guy is guilty," they scream at me, "so why are you helping him?"

At times an investigator can help neither himself nor his clients. That's the nature of this business.

TIPS FOR POTENTIAL WITNESSES

1. *What should you do if you don't wish to talk to an investigator?* An obvious but incorrect answer is to refuse to do so. If the investigator senses your reluctance, he will find a way to compel you to talk. This may include an elaborate subterfuge and possibly a subpoena. You may well end up wasting a day or two in front of a judge or in an attorney's office under stressful, mandatory deposition. Those who have been a pain in the rear for investigators will find that their time and previous schedules—including weekends and vacation time—are intentionally, vigorously trashed. Nineteen times out of twenty, casual witnesses will find they never hear of or see the investigator again after their brief 10- to 20-minute conversation. As a practical matter, cooperation—even if it is half-hearted, phony cooperation—is far cheaper, easier, and quicker than resistance.

   If you are suspicious of an investigator, you should talk to him but keep your answers short, vague, and bereft of details—and be sure not to let down your guard as the interview winds down!

2. *What about alibis?* Knowing exactly what you or an acquaintance did three weeks ago on Tuesday night is virtually impossible for average, law-abiding people. Investigators know this. Alibis can work, but only if they are very general, filled with "I can't recalls" or "I don't knows," and generally conform to what investigators will find on the ground when they go check. People

usually can't recall or substantiate an alibi stretching back several weeks unless something unique occurred at that same time. It is better to say, "I think maybe I was watching the History Channel that night. . . . What programs? . . . I have no clue!"

Witnesses who display perfect recall are usually assumed to be lying or covering up something important. Investigators are suspicious of detailed, she-said/he-said alibis and will check them out thoroughly. If you send an investigator to corroborate a false alibi, your house of cards may tumble, and you may find yourself in front of a judge or worse.

3. If you are being interrogated by a police officer, you might start things off by asking about his sales experience. Make small talk, throw his timing off, and you will learn what you are really up against if he tells you the truth (which is very unlikely).

4. Don't be fooled by "hidden" evidence tactics.

5. Don't agree to the video or audio taping of the interview.

6. Do ask for names of other people being interviewed for this case. You might even ask the investigator what legal issues are involved. This always causes the investigator to stop and think.

7. Always find out which side the investigator is working for. His answer may be evasive, but it doesn't hurt to ask—though few witnesses do.

THE FINE ARTS OF LISTENING AND OBSERVING

LISTENING AND OBSERVING ARE LOST SKILLS in our modern society. This is true in spite of the fact that some of us spend up to 12 hours a day listening to and watching the one-eyed brain destroyer. Some smart old codgers maintain that for every hour a person watches television, he loses an IQ point. This situation of passive, noncognitive listening and observing has become so pervasive in our society that people are shocked and sometimes upset when they encounter people who really do listen and observe.

WHAT DOES LISTENING REALLY ENTAIL?

Listening means carefully and meticulously training ourselves to hear exactly what people are saying. There's nothing magical about this! TV commentators often interpret what someone said, but no interpreter is needed when we do the job for ourselves. All that is needed is for us to listen to *what is said*—not what we wanted or expected the person to say.

Using Nonverbal Clues

At times nonverbal clues such as eye or hand movements, body posture, or facial expressions will either reinforce or contradict what is being said. Truly observant investigators will pick these up. But, alas, most of us listen only to the extent that we buy time to formulate our next response, which is often specifically designed to impress the other guy by making us look super cool, wise, or perceptive (whether we really are or not). And so we tend to miss these important clues, as well as much of what is actually being said.

Asking Questions

Those who wish to test their listening ability should try going to their next social outing as listeners. Try listening to what other people are saying to the exclusion of everything else. Then these "listeners" should question their subjects till it is clear what they really mean. When their meaning is not clear or there is an opportunity to learn about the cotton futures markets, the diamond cartel, or factory production of ax handles, for instance, ask precise, pointed questions. One very good investigator makes it his policy at otherwise dull parties to ask, "What exactly do you do during an average day?" People should be wary of guys like him. This chap has the reputation of being one of the brightest, most outgoing people in the area. He blatantly practices the fine art of the "five Ws." People know it, and they still enjoy being around him.

Rather than thinking of you as a fool for asking so many questions, people will either come to believe that you are the most intelligent person at the party or suspect other motives. Perhaps suspicion is not common, but it is what goes through my mind under the uncommon circumstance of finding a real listener who, I suspect, is also an observer.

Keeping the Conversation Going

What should you do when the conversation lags? Repeat the last statement made to you, but phrase it as a question. This technique is corny and sometimes transparent to some, but usually a miracle occurs when it is practiced. People will start explaining their entire life history in minute detail. This may sound boring, but it is not wasted effort. All investigators have turned up people with unique talents whom they later call upon to help with their investigations. The people are flattered, the clients are impressed, and all is done at minimum cost. For example, over the Christmas holidays, I discovered a husband and wife who raised and worked sled dogs. Principally because he was so jacked up about my interest in him, he jumped into an animal damage case with such enthusiasm that I eventually had to back him off a bit.

Putting Your Skills to the Test

For a time I worked with the chief inspector of the Illinois State Police. He's retired now, so I can tell this story. He and his fellow investigators used to play a little game with each other when they went to social functions outside their official sphere. The challenge was to find out the bra size of as many women at the party as possible. The one with the most information won. Guessing was not allowed. The woman or her husband had to reveal exact information, or it didn't count. The investigators were on their honor, and, of course, they cross-checked their information. By the way, this was the Midwest, not Hollywood, so getting this information really was tough. The first guy to approach a woman could always deploy a pretext about a free swimsuit, but what the others did is beyond me. I personally had no chance in that contest. (More about pretexts in Chapter 3.)

OBSERVING IS MORE THAN SEEING

Like listening, observance is learned. Becoming super-observant is entirely a matter of training and practice. One novice investigator used to put a very small pebble in his shoe. Every time he stepped on the pebble he reminded himself to observe brands of cigarettes or cigars, booze, watches, brands of suits, colors of vehicles, condition of clothes, hands, hats, shoes, and whatever else. Soon it was such fun and he was sufficiently conditioned that he removed the stone. But he found he also had to continually remind himself to listen as well as observe.

Sir Arthur Conan Doyle in "A Scandal in Bohemia," a short story in *The Adventures of Sherlock Holmes,* used the example of Watson's not knowing the number of steps that led from one room to another to show how unobservant most people are.

> "When I hear you give your reasons," [Watson] remarked, "the thing always appears to me to be so ridiculously simple that I could easily do it myself, though at each successive instance of your reasoning I am baffled until you explain your process. And yet I believe that my eyes are as good as yours."
>
> "Quite so," [Holmes] answered, lighting a cigarette, and throwing himself down into an armchair. "You see, but you do not observe. This distinction is clear. For example, you have frequently seen the steps which lead up from the hall to this room."
>
> "Frequently."
>
> "How often?"
>
> "Well, hundreds of times."
>
> "How many are there?"
>
> "How many? I don't know."
>
> "Quite so! You have not observed. And yet you have seen. That is just my point. Now, I know that there are seventeen steps, because I have both seen and observed."

Perhaps this fictional example doesn't seem useful—after all, why would people need to know how many steps lead to another room?—but how many of us learn to observe rings, tattoos, scars, whether people can read or write, or whether their hands are those of a laborer or an office worker?

USING SILENCE TO LISTEN AND OBSERVE

Those who are reading this book for defensive purposes because they wish to outfox an investigator should keep in mind that great investigators/interrogators have an unusual ability to listen and observe. Many of them do this by deploying silence to their advantage. Worse even than encountering a listener, Americans cannot stand silence once they start talking about themselves. Japanese businessmen who use silence as a negotiating tool frequently hack their American counterparts to ribbons. The Japanese just sit there without saying a word, eventually taking all the marbles.

EVALUATING THE LISTENING
AND OBSERVATION SKILLS OF OTHERS

It is a little known and infrequently reported fact, but one of the duties of a private investigator involves evaluating the listening abilities, as well as social proclivities, of anyone involved in their cases. Well-financed clients who are determined to win spend really big bucks finding out how well potential jurors listen, their educational levels, how much they have traveled, what they do for a living, and, if possible, their religious and social biases.

On the basis of this information, jurors judged to be favorable to the client are selected. As long as investigators openly talk to friends and acquaintances about potential jurors' background and biases and do not attempt to influence them about that specific case, it is not considered jury tampering.

Absolutely astounding numbers of potential jurors must be evaluated. This checking is never quick, simple, or cheap. Everything must be done before selection and impaneling. Most investigators figure $20,000 to evaluate a list of 100 potential jurors. Clients must want to win very badly and have very deep pockets to pull this off.

KINESICS INTERVIEWING

Kinesics interviewing is the art of evaluating body language in an effort to determine truth or falsehood. Kinesics studies nonverbal body motions such as eye movements, shrugging, crossing and uncrossing of the legs, touching, pointing, and hand movements to suggest whether the person being interviewed is lying or telling the truth. The system relies heavily on investigators with great observation and listening abilities. Investigators using kinesics must be patient, capable of negotiating from silence, and able to continually ask the correct questions in such a way that the interviewee is forced to consider the ramifications and implications of his answers.

Note carefully that this technique is referred to as an art, not a science. Most investigators who use kinesics maintain that it is not a hard science because it cannot be tested and replicated. Some witnesses by their very nature just will not look strangers in the eye, or they become nervous, crossing and uncrossing their legs, without any deep-seated larcenous intent.

Therein lies the failing of kinesics for many investigators. A benchmark must be established for each individual, and this takes a great deal of time. Some investigators try to get around to eight or ten potential witnesses per day. Just talking to and establishing rapport with all these folks is difficult enough without trying to establish a point of reference relative to their individual body movements. A valid kinesics evaluation takes at least two or three hours. If the subject of the interview is a hardened criminal or an experienced witness, the interview must be much longer.

Kinesics is the trendy stepchild of witness interviewing and cycles in and out of favor on a regular basis. In real life there is definitely a place for kinesics evaluation, but investigators must be trained to use it properly. Some witnesses are naturally shifty looking, cannot establish eye contact, and do a poor job of representing their case on the stand. Good private investigators highlight these characteristics in their reports to clients so that these people will not be called as witnesses.

As with many investigators, I have made only nominal use of kinesics. If a witness will talk to me straight out after hearing my reason for wanting information and he has no other obvious biases, I usually assume he is telling the truth. For instance, asking a witness if he observed open cans or bottles of booze at a crash site usually will elicit a truthful response. Most citizens are happy to help. Either they recall such action, or they do not. (Of course, an investigator has a duty to evaluate possible biases, but more about that later.)

Police investigators who use grueling eight- or ten-hour interrogations tend to put more faith in reading body language than fast-moving private investigators. We will address this issue in Chapter 5 on criminal investigations, but often cops make it so easy and tempting to confess that they sometimes drag confessions that aren't necessarily accurate out of people.

TIPS FOR POTENTIAL WITNESSES

1. Do not be deceived by an investigator's use of silence. This is a deliberate technique designed to make you uncomfortable enough to start talking—and keep talking until you have spilled everything.
2. If an investigator starts repeating your last statement in the form of a question, just remain silent. Do not start explaining what you meant or adding more details.
3. Listen carefully to the questions and provide only specific answers to them—do not provide more than what's being asked.
4. Make eye contact, do not cross your arms or legs, showing a defensive posture.
5. Be especially quiet and cautious around a person who is obviously a listener and observer. This won't keep him from getting a lot of information, but it might keep you from giving away the store.
6. Try to maintain one posture without much "body language." For some people in some cultures this is impossible. Don't worry—few investigators rely heavily on kinesics unless the witness is obvious about it.

3

WHAT ARE PRETEXTS AND HOW ARE THEY USED?

DEVELOPING A VALID REASON FOR HOSTILE, openly suspicious witnesses to spill their guts is absolutely the heart and soul of all witness interrogations. In the business, these reasons are called pretexts. Witnesses aren't going to give out very much good information unless they can be convinced that they should actively want to tell the investigator everything they know. Many people in the industry believe that a reference manual that will help with this process, or that will get them thinking about the use of investigators' pretexts, is easily worth its weight in gold!

Virtually every situation an investigator faces is different. But it is universally known that top investigators are nearly impossible for witnesses to resist simply because they are masters at devising that one reason in the whole wide world for a witness to do or say something about the situa-

29

tion at hand. In most cases regular citizens have no clue what they are doing or saying as they are cleverly drawn into telling everything they know.

Again, let the record note that good investigators are extremely, fantastically clever at thinking up reasons for witnesses to tell all. This one quality alone is usually the single most important characteristic of a really good, experienced investigator. Even poor listeners who invent brilliant pretexts can be successful. Sorry about this repetition, but casual readers can never imagine how much time I have spent thinking up pretexts for typically hostile people to tell me stuff.

To get people to confess or tell them things, criminal investigators use a variation of a pretext where they must also think up some person or thing they can lead a suspect into blaming for his or her unlawful predicament. "You shoplifted the expensive jewelry and clothes because your mother was too tight and mean to buy them for you" is a common one for those investigators who work loss prevention for retailers. Experienced police interrogators tell me that they blame the lawbreakers' parents or the victims themselves if nothing better comes to mind after the first hour of interrogation—"You stole from the guy because he was such a rich, arrogant bastard and that's okay."

PRETEXTS FOR SECURING FINANCIAL INFORMATION

One of the most common uses of pretexts by private investigators is to secure information from a person's financial or employment records. Numerous times during the year I get calls from people who want me to find out how much money a defendant has in his bank account. "Had an investigator who just went tappety-tap a few seconds on his computer and came up with the balance," they frequently tell me, after I explain that securing this information is difficult and costly.

Three methods exist for securing individual and corporate bank account information: (1) schmooze (use pretexts and some occasional cash) low-level tellers, wives, or secretaries into revealing the bank where the account is secured and amount; (2) salvage bank information from the trash; and (3) surreptitiously check out the subject's office or mailbox for bank statements. This last method is not recommended. Contrary to TV information, this method it is seldom successful. The closest most investigators have come using this method is to be standing in a target's office or home on another pretext near the checkbook, which they quickly peruse. Recently I was able to make off with a blank check from the office of a company running a platinum scam that I was investigating. However, it was something of a hollow victory, as the secretary had already told me the information I was able to acquire by having the blank check (that the company had $465 in the U.S. Bank in town). All three methods generally require the use of pretexts.

Should the Pretext be Delivered by Phone or in Person?

Evidence suggests that good investigators, both private and civil, can and do work successful pretexts both through personal contacts and the phone. Most prefer one method or the other but can do both.

One factor that helps determine which to use is the witness to be interviewed. Several classes of witnesses exist. Some have only bits of information such as "He was here last night watching TV" or "You will find her at 331 Monroe" or "He works at McDonald's." Others witnesses may be experts at the business under discussion and can assist with a general understanding of what is going on or with specific knowledge about what you are investigating. All witnesses should be treated individually in terms of pretexts and whether it's best to interview on the phone, call to arrange an in-person interview, or just show up for the interview.

Personal-contact types stress that they catch witnesses unaware and without a rehearsed story when they show up unannounced and unexpected on the witnesses' doorstep or at their workplace. During personal contacts, outstanding investigators know how to keep things going until they have wrung the witness dry of information. As we discussed in the previous chapter, most honest investigators—both public and private, on the phone or in person—will admit that they get 40 to 60 percent of the good stuff out of people after they have said, "The interview is over, thanks very much." It all comes out in a rushing torrent after the witness lets down his guard.

On the other hand, investigators who prefer working the phones can also incorporate an element of surprise. They also claim that they can fake more documents from which to quote to the witness. These bogus documents can range from alleged copies of military discharge papers to loan papers to employment applications.

A favorite trick of investigators to secure usable bank account information is the two-step "rebate check" pretext. Investigators send the target a "product rebate" check for $20, which is usually deposited in his bank account and then returned to the account on which the check was drawn. Having the bank name and account number (which can often—but not always—be deduced from the returned canceled check) provides the investigator with the information needed to call the bank about "his" account to verify the balances, or he can run the common "Is this check good?" pretext. Here's an example:

"Hello, this is Ralph Lee from All-Star Auto here in town, and your Mr. Williams wants to put a check for $3,000 down on one of our used trucks, which he insists on driving away."

"Oh, funds in the account won't cover it," you say in response to the bank's refusal. "I'm glad I took a minute to call. Thank you for being so helpful, but hold on a second more."

Coming back to the phone, you tell the bank clerk, "Mr. Williams says he will write a check for $2,000 and finance the balance. Mr. Williams says I am supposed to tell you that you had damn well better cover that much."

Often if you have been light, delightful, and believable with the bank clerk, she will confide that Mr. Williams' account couldn't cover a $100 check and that you had better be careful. You then offer to send the bank clerk a box of candy because she just saved you thousands of dollars. You tell your client you got the information by computer to cover your ass. But 99 percent of the time, it is done with sophisticated two- or three-part pretexts.

Preemployment Check Pretext

Another commonly employed phone pretext used to gather financial information on a subject is the preemployment background check. For instance, if I detect that a previous employer is hesitant or hostile, I will tell him, "It says here on her employment application that you paid her two grand a week. Given the type of people I usually check out, two grand is perhaps four times a reasonable salary." Usually I don't even have an employment application in front of me, but the person I'm talking to doesn't know that.

Often this approach gets previous employers going so hard and fast and with such passion that I have trouble writing it all down and then nicely shutting them up. Responses range from "Wow, we didn't pay near that much" to "She was just a crummy waitress, what do you think I am, stupid?" to "She stole cigarettes and beer so we canned her." Sometimes, but not often, when dealing with an honest worker, I am asked, "Why do you suppose she told you that? Normally, she is a very honest person."

The preemployment check is one of those perfect pretexts that has an element of truth, so it sounds plausible to the witness.

I have never heard of an investigator getting into legal trouble over the use of these types of pretexts. Many cover their behinds by using pretexts as close to the truth as possible. The use of pretexts by police investigators has been tested in court. The courts have determined that it doesn't matter what the police officers say; what matters is what the witness, the accused, the victim—you pick it—says!

Why I Prefer Pretexts to Computer Databases

Although little difference exists between investigators who favor telephones and those who favor personal interviews for pretexts, there is an insurmountable gulf between people-type pretext users and "computer nerds." I don't believe I have ever encountered a face-to-face, effective people person who is also a computer nerd. A combination of both skills is indeed rare. A computer expert's creativity is totally different.

Without doubt a great deal of information is available on the Internet, with new or expanded data banks appearing almost daily. In my experience, however, most do not deliver very much specific information, especially given the time and money invested.

Let the record note, I am not a computer person. Readers should take this evaluation with a grain of salt, but it seems to me that computers are slow, difficult to manipulate successfully, and expensive, and they frequently provide only partial information.

Costs, even at $5 per file, soon mount up as you try various spellings of names, different middle initials, and other variations in an attempt to get the right information from these data banks. An acid test is to attempt to locate information on yourself in various data banks. The results of my test have always been raggedy. My wife is something of a computer nerd, so when I say I can usually get better, quicker, more complete information using pretexts than computers, it is based on actual experience.

Some information that is part of the daily work investigators do can never be secured from computers. For instance, computers can't tell you a wife's experience at her husband's hand when she is trying to break his last will and testament. Nor will they explain what students and parents

Private investigators fall into two categories: those good at mining computer databanks for information and those who are more effective dealing with people face-to-face or on the phone.

saw as a drunk fan chased an old man away from a basketball game and beat him up badly.

TAILOR PRETEXTS TO THE INDIVIDUAL

Good pretexts are tailored specifically for the person to whom they are directed, do not reveal their real intent, and have as much truth in them as possible. Not only are more truthful pretexts more desirable, they are easier for investigators to remember and execute. I have even gone to the trouble of writing a story about an incident after posing as a reporter/writer in an attempt to interject honesty and believability into a pretext—an especially helpful prop if I have to go back for more information.

Two of my favorite pretexts are as follows:

- "The judge sent me out to find out what is really going on. My report will be available to everyone involved in this issue. I will even send you one if you wish." Most of the time witnesses don't want a copy of the report, and they very seldom write down my name and telephone number. I rarely give out a false name, for that matter, or am asked for a business card with my real name.

- "I am a private investigator working for the insurance company so it can do what is fair and right in this case." I frequently tell this to people who are reluctant to talk. Contrary to popular opinion, insurance companies are still held in some regard, at least in my neck of the woods.

A simple little tackle box with a few odds and ends often becomes the prop for a pretext I might use when searching for someone. A common scenario would be as follows: "Found this at the lake with Mr. Brown's name and address," says I to his mother (or whomever I'm trying to get information from).

"Just leave it here and I will see he gets it," she responds.

"Oh, no, see, he has a whatamathingy lure with moose feather topping that I have only observed in Iceland, and I want to talk personally with the fellow about how he got the lure and how it works in these waters," I reply.

"But I didn't know he even went fishing," says she.

"Well, there is a condom in the tackle box so maybe there is something else. Just tell me where to take it and I will do so."

Usually this last little twist gets everyone going, and I locate my hidden witness.

NEGATIVE PRETEXTS

Some pretexts are negative. "I won't talk to you at all," a woman recently shouted at me in her place of employment. "Okay," I replied, "I will talk to everyone in the neighborhood and your workplace about the incident. Someone is bound to recall what you told him." Then she had to worry about my picking up biased information, which could become a personal problem for her.

I have also threatened to go to a potential witness' parents, employer, or debt holder, or to consult their criminal record if they fail to cooperate. Normal people don't want strangers mucking around in their private affairs. With this threat, the witness usually is either scared silly or horribly belligerent. Pulling this pretext on someone likely to become belligerent is not recommended, reinforcing the principle that all pretexts must be carefully crafted for specific situations. When another pretext isn't available, this admittedly blunt instrument sometimes works, but it all depends on the person and circumstance.

With traumatized witnesses I throw out the line that "we could have worked all of this out in a five- to ten-minute talk, but obviously you have something to hide." Usually I get an interview. Of course, it takes far longer than five to ten minutes to do an interview, but being interviewed for most people is like taking the first bite of peanuts. Once they start, they just can't stop.

TRY A LITTLE FRIENDLINESS

Friendly, gregarious, outgoing investigators have a great advantage when using pretexts. If you can gain the witness' confidence with good, solid pretexts, you will usually carry the day. In this regard, honey always works better than vinegar, as we'll see throughout this book!

As discussed, a successful investigator must be able to think up effective pretexts tailored to specific people or circumstances. Studying examples of pretexts used by others is as fine as frog hair when used to get your juices going, but don't be surprised if there is little specific carryover to your exact situation. With that said, the following five real-life examples might help you come up with your own pretexts.

"IT'S OKAY" PRETEXT

The "everything will be okay if you just confess" pretext

is frequently used when interviewing teenage girls caught shoplifting. "It's okay," I will tell them. "Just return the merchandise, confess, and ask for forgiveness, and we will let you go." Investigators cannot really scarch thcsc suspected shoplifters without potential legal problems, and rough talk and intimidation are also forbidden. But this little pretext gets about 80 percent of them, and if they are visibly scared when placed under detention, it *always* works. Usually I have them confess to the store manager, but, believe it or not, soft-hearted store managers usually let these girls go without pressing charges.

Police interviewers often use the pretext that "whatever you did is not really so bad—my wife's brother did exactly the same thing, and he didn't get in trouble" to get otherwise reluctant witnesses to explain exactly what happened.

Claiming that what happened was "an act of God, fate, or an accident, so don't worry about it" is another effective pretext. "Just tell me how this happened to occur" is a variation of "Everybody is doing it; it's no big deal, so relax and fill me in on what exactly transpired."

GOOD-COP/BAD-COP PRETEXT

Another great pretext uses the "good-cop/bad-cop" routine. I frequently tell people I am just a nonthreatening private investigator with no real power or interest in the outcome. "Let's get this settled out before the big, tough, bad guys take over with their court summons and police and search warrants," I often say. At the same time, I give an impression of actually being mild-mannered and reasonable, rather than wild-eyed and radical. This can be expanded if appropriate by alternating between "I could care less" and "Let's talk before the big kids get here" pretexts. "Just talk to me two minutes so we can get this dumb problem behind us," I often say.

USING "HYPOTHETICAL" PRETEXTS

Asking witnesses what they would have done hypothetically under the same circumstances often cuts right to the heart of a matter. Recently, I was unsure whether a client was obviously drunk when involved in an accident. I asked the witnesses to the accident what they would have done if they had been the driver in the situation my client found himself in. Everyone said they would not have been drinking and driving or carrying dozens of empty beer cans around in the car with them. Without asking outright if there were any signs of booze, I knew I had the honest, correct answer.

Skilled interviewers know they will always get something from a witness as long as they keep him talking. Quite often investigators encounter people who, probably on the advice of their attorneys, keep repeating, "I have absolutely nothing to say to you!" When this happens to me, I say, "I am sorry. What did I say that upset you so much? Please tell me so that I can better talk to the next person. I do not view myself as a mean, nasty guy. I don't want to offend the next person." This works about 50 percent of the time.

SITUATIONAL PRETEXTS

Situational pretexts are commonly used in child-snatching cases. These are actually variations of pretexts cops use to get petty criminals to come, for example, to a clothing store to get their free suit, Levis, sweater, or whatever. When the suckers turn up, they are arrested. I have found missing kids by showing grandma a bogus scholarship certificate, health notice, government recall notice, or whatever. "Mama and Junior need to come to such and such an address to respond," I explain to the grandma. Often, my phone rings, or they come knocking at my door.

Lists of potential pretexts can be as long as an investigator's list of clients. Each pretext is tailored specifically to give unsuspecting witnesses a reason to talk. I firmly believe that if pretexts are properly used by real experts, few people can resist telling all.

ARE PRETEXTS IMMORAL OR UNETHICAL?

Is the use of pretexts immoral or unethical? For the most part, dealing with biased witnesses or even those who have formed an opinion is an immoral business. It would be nice to be able to go to such a person and say, "You owe this amount. How much do you really have in your bank account?" "What really happened that night in the parking lot?" "Where is the kid"? "Really, truly, how disabled are you?" But the people with whom I deal are never that forthcoming.

I liken it to a basketball or football game where faking out the opposition is expected and accepted. The people you interview are trying to fake you out, but you are smarter and have the initiative.

To understand a real master of the use of pretexts, read about King David in 1 and 2 Samuel and Kings in the Old Testament. King David was a master at the pretext business. Pretexts flew like wild pigeons in his case!

• • •

The following are examples of investigations from real life. They illustrate a number of pretexts employed successfully to get at the truth.

REAL-LIFE EXAMPLE ONE

On-the-ground situation:
Your client wants you to locate a specific material wit-

ness. This witness knows you are after him and doesn't want to get involved or testify against a buddy. (This pretext can be used on the phone or at the home of a family member or close friend of the witness.)

Pretext:

"Hi, I'm Duncan Farnsworth from the Farmers Alliance Insurance Company. I have a cashier's check here for $7,821.30 in full settlement of Mr. Smith's wrongful discharge claim.

"Sorry, I don't know exactly what this money is for, I suspect because he was improperly fired at his last job. I have to deliver it to Mr. Smith personally so he can sign for it. He can cash the check at any bank.

"Was he fired from a job last year? I guess the money is for that deal, but I really don't know," I continue.

Result:

Almost everyone is sufficiently greedy to try to get their hands on an alleged check for almost eight grand. This pretext seldom fails. I use it often.

REAL-LIFE EXAMPLE TWO

On-the-ground situation:

Three rowdy teens, who were probably drinking, pulled dangerously close behind your client's vehicle. They followed it down the highway for 20 miles, harassing her with obscenities. Your client later called the police, but they wouldn't do anything. She has decided to sue the teens. Your job is to interview the kids to listen to their side of the story and, as closely as possible, discover the truth about what really happened. In this case, you need to talk to the three teens and find out what they think about what went on, as well as whether they bragged to their friends about their actions. Who are their friends? Obviously, the defendants or their friends won't want to talk to an investigator from the "other side" while a civil action is pending. I call or visit the kids' parents with this pretext.

Pretext:
"I am an investigator for attorney Stoney Heart in Ashton. He is handling the XYZ case, as I am certain you know. Mr. Heart has taken some really bad cases recently, which he lost big time. He is very fearful that this might be another of those circumstances. Professionally, he cannot afford to take another hit. Could you please ask your kids to tell me what really happened in this situation, so that we can make a decision how to proceed?"

Result:
Nine times out of ten the parents of kids who are in trouble view this reasonable approach as a prelude to their talking their way out of the suit and will agree to talk. Then it's my duty as the investigator to get them to spill their guts.

REAL-LIFE EXAMPLE THREE

On-the-ground situation:
A female employee successfully embezzled significant funds from her employer, who is just starting to figure out exactly how much she made off with. He wants me to find out the magnitude of her skimming and in which bank, if any, she keeps the ill-gotten funds. I call up the employee.

Pretext:
"Hello, this is Stuart Straight. I understand from a mutual acquaintance (supply an appropriate name) that you are looking for funds to start a new business. I am a man of considerable financial means who is always looking for new

business opportunities in which to invest. Can we meet to talk about business opportunities?"

After protracted small talk, I agree to put up nine dollars for each one of hers. "I want you to cry little tears if I have to cry big tears," I explain. "All that is needed is proof of your ability to go forward."

Result:

The embezzler views this as yet another opportunity to "clean out" a business partner's bank account. In some cases I may open a joint bank account where she deposits her funds. I clean this out for my client, or to avoid charges of fraud, give the necessary information to my client and let him run a writ on the account.

REAL-LIFE EXAMPLE FOUR

On-the-ground situation:

The manager of a relatively large local store comes to me regarding theft of old used scrap iron from his business. As the story unfolded, the missing items were so insignificant that I could not believe he wanted to proceed. It was the difference between the items going to the landfill or an employee's garage. Either action accomplished the same objective: to get them out of the store. But he was adamant, so I screened the employees—19, as I recall. As the story unfolded, an unexpected hidden agenda was uncovered, which often makes this line of work interesting and enjoyable.

Pretext:

Using my generic business card, I approach all of the key employees in the store with the pretext that I am starting another retail operation in the city and actively looking for good employees.

I ask only two questions: "Would you consider moving to

my store if the pay were slightly more than you currently receive?" and "What do you personally believe should be done with employees who steal from their employer?"

(Of course, it isn't universal, but people who believe they might be in trouble with their employer will consider leaving. It is universally true that people who have been doing something wrong tend to wish that their behavior be reviewed with charity and understanding. Guilty people almost always say, "Employees who steal should be sent to counseling," or "It all depends on the extent of their larceny." Honest employees usually react indignantly: "Those who steal while in a place of trust should be rigorously prosecuted.")

Result:
A day later, the store manager announced to his employees that a private investigator wished to talk to some of them about thefts from the store. Two days after that he scheduled an appointment for the following day with three employees who I had determined might be the culprits based on their answers in the first part of the interview. The three-day interval was calculated to give the culprits time to worry.

Less than five minutes into the first of these interviews my phone rings. A female voice (who wasn't one of my three suspects) says I should stop searching, that she had stolen the scrap iron as a means of embarrassing her department head. Here is where the hidden agenda comes in. It seems her department head is a full-blown practicing lesbian who has been hitting on her. This woman only wanted to expose, embarrass, and discredit her boss. Strange business, this.

REAL-LIFE EXAMPLE FIVE

On-the-ground situation:
A relatively young woman claims that she received a disabling shock from her electric range. Ten thousand dollars

would make her whole again, she informs my client's insurance company. Of course, fraud is suspected, but ten grand is not that much money. The company is *almost* ready to pay, just to make this all go away. But before it does, I am asked to investigate to see if I can uncover anything.

Pretext:

While interviewing the woman, I sense that she is uncomfortable with her allegations. She doesn't say so, but I get the impression that all this is her husband's idea, and she is a bit afraid of what might happen. This helps me select my pretext. Gradually, I explain it is okay to make false claims, as long as she comes to realize that they are false and that she eventually confesses and asks for forgiveness.

Result:

After about 60 minutes, the woman confesses that her disability claims are untrue, and she begins asking for forgiveness. I tell her all will be forgiven and everything will be okay if she also confesses to the insurance adjuster. We call him on the phone, and she quickly blows her case right out the stack without really realizing what she is doing.

Subsequently no insurance money was paid. But I did hear later that her husband beat her up and threw her out over the incident.

TIPS FOR POTENTIAL WITNESSES

1. Always ask for a name and phone number and a business card before beginning any personal interview with an investigator. This simple strategy forestalls a great many pretexts.
2. Don't be persuaded to talk about anything "hypothetical."
3. Don't fall for any "free" offers. Often these are pretexts designed to catch you off guard.
4. Remember to keep your guard up until the interview is completely over. You don't want to blow it at the very end.
5. Ask to see any documents the investigator refers to before commenting—they may be fake.
6. Don't fall for the "it's OK" or the "good cop/bad cop" pretext.
7. Again, always ask who the investigator represents, and take your own notes.
8. Don't allow an investigator into your office or house, where correspondence, financial papers (check books, letters from banks, etc.) may be lying around. Even books may tip off an alert investigator to your character or intentions.
9. Protecting financial information is really difficult. A good investigator will get this no matter what countermeasures you take.

CIVIL VS. CRIMINAL PROCEEDINGS AND RULES OF EVIDENCE

OF THOSE CITIZENS WHO BECOME ENSNARED in the court system, 98 percent will be involved with either criminal or civil courts; the remaining 2 percent could be involved with patent courts, tribal courts, or another specialized court. Criminal actions entail violations of a government statute for which one is charged by "the state." Civil actions involve allegations of wrongful activities leading to damages that are claimed in reparation by the party allegedly wronged, the plaintiff. Plainly put, criminal charges could simply be characterized as "you were caught breaking the law." A civil action could be interpreted as "you hurt me, and now I want to be made well again by you." From an investigative point of view, there is often (but not always) something of a difference between the two.

Criminal cases are investigated for the prosecution by the

police in close cooperation with the prosecuting attorney. Criminal defendants who have the necessary funds and who believe they can prove their innocence may hire private investigators to research their side of the issue. A sharp, quick investigation can often bolster a good defense, but as a practical matter, criminal defendants seldom have sufficient funds to hire attorneys, let alone investigators! A significant number of criminal cases are handled by public defenders because the defendants are broke.

Wisdom within the trade alleges that, in most cases, those with public defenders will be pled away *by their own counsel* as quickly and quietly as possible, regardless of the merits of their case. This conventional wisdom contends that public defenders actively pursue only high-profile cases. For instance, I recently investigated a public defender in eastern Washington state who seldom—if ever—opened her clients' files until she walked down the hall with them into court. Until three minutes before court, she had no idea of what her clients were even accused of. With her as their counsel, experienced criminals who could argue their own cases often had the best chance. Hers is admittedly an extreme example, but it suggests that there is often little defense from public defenders in general. (For the record, this lawyer is now disbarred.)

Having criminal charges filed against them is usually disastrous for average citizens. Many ultimately prove their innocence but irretrievably lose their entire family and personal fortune in the process. My rule of thumb is that every American should have at least $15,000 in instant cash with which to ward off spurious legal actions they will likely face.

A recent countervailing trend in the industry provides a ray of hope for destitute citizens facing criminal charges who, because of limited finances, must depend on a public defender. For some, but not all, truly heinous crimes (including homicide and rape), some modern courts appoint and fund private investigators for the indigent accused. This investigator's job is to act as a type of counterbalance to the state's investigators, whose resources often overwhelm those of public defenders. Hiring a private investigator to assist the public defender is also seen as a way the state can reduce the possibility of costly appeals later. By investigating the case thoroughly before the trial, the state faces less likelihood that the defendant can later appeal on the grounds that the public defender did an inadequate job of representing him. In other words, judges seem to reason that, if the state spends $3,000 now for an investigator, it will save 10 times as much later on in avoided appeals and delays on the same case.

Criminal verdicts are always decided by unanimous vote of 12 jurors. At times jurors may negotiate among themselves to reach a lesser verdict, but always the 12 must agree. Civil verdicts are established by the rules of the state in which these actions are filed. For example, some states require only nine jurors to agree to find for or against in a civil case, while others require the verdict to be unanimous. In those states where the decision does not have to be unanimous, it is generally conceded that civil plaintiffs have a more attainable goal.

Everyone is on their own in civil court; there are no public defenders or investigators. I have had clients involved in situations that were a mix of civil and criminal action who complained that they would not have needed to hire me if the police had done their work. All one receives from the state in civil matters is a set of procedural rules, a judge, a jury, a courtroom, record keeping, and enforcement of any court decisions. Most private investigative and expert witness work today is done in conjunction with civil matters.

Rules of evidence among states and between criminal and civil actions vary dramatically. For instance, in two of the states in which I work, I cannot legally record an interview without the interviewee's express permission. In the third I can legally record away, with only one party's (my own) consent to the recording. Because these rules are often arcane and difficult, many states require that private investigators both pass an examination and have a set amount of experience before they are approved for work in that state.

Why would an investigator record an interview? Because witnesses frequently change their testimony. I recently encountered a female witness in an alleged sexual harassment case who indicated a willingness to appear on behalf of the plaintiff. The two women were co-workers in what I would characterize as a pretty sleazy bar. The would-be witness was a very "handsome woman"—far better looking than her friend who was alleging sexual harassment against the owner of the bar—so interviewing her for my client, the bar owner, was definitely more interesting than interviewing average scuzzball males! During the interview, the witness admitted that the plaintiff had offered her part of the anticipated money settlement in exchange for favorable testimony. She also admitted that she had never been harassed—sexually or otherwise—by the defendant, and that she had never seen the defendant harass anyone or take any improper actions toward any of his employees.

But my side remained skeptical to the last about her. Like police in that state, I recorded every word she said in case she changed her story yet again. We couldn't use the recording as evidence in court, but I could appear as an expert witness to impeach her testimony. My recording was used as a reference to replicate her comments during my testimony. It helped me get ready to take the stand and swear that what she told me was different from what she testified in court. But that was unnecessary—she eventually came through like a champ, telling the same version she had told me.

DIRECT VS. HEARSAY EVIDENCE

In most courts, investigators are not allowed to officially report evidence given to them by witnesses they have interviewed. Unless it is a deathbed testimony of some sort that cannot be replicated from the witness himself, investigators cannot testify. Information told to investigators by witnesses is hearsay evidence unless it is used to impeach testimony.

Why do investigators spend so much time looking for witnesses when they cannot validly report their testimony in court? By succinctly summarizing statements made by witnesses; providing information on how these people can be reached when needed; and characterizing their honesty, their biases, their reluctance or eagerness to appear in court, and what kind of spoken and visual impression they convey, private investigators can greatly assist the attorney, cut expenses, and provide another angle of thought on the matter. Private investigators usually work for one-third the cost of attorneys, so they can do the investigative work more cheaply—as well as more quickly— than attorneys who try to do the job themselves.

As mentioned, rules vary a bit state to state, but expect that testimony about direct evidence by a witness will be admissible. "I saw her ram the knife into his chest three or four times" is a good example of testimony about direct evidence. Indirect evidence does not prove a fact or event, but implies or presumes that this evidence is true: "I heard him scream and then saw her walking off carrying a bloody knife—she had blood up to her elbows." Indirect evidence is not seen as conclusive but is often used as a means of substantiating an already obvious act (e.g., photos of the victim's dead body displaying multiple stab wounds).

EXPERT TESTIMONY

In U.S. courts, expert opinions tend to be scientific in nature. Experts in loss prevention can testify about the ease with which a store's merchandise can be shoplifted, but an investigator who caught a shoplifter with stolen goods can only say, "I caught her with the following items." Medical doctors, plumbers, psychiatrists, vehicle reconstructionists, and just about anyone under the correct circumstances can be an expert witness.

PRIVILEGED COMMUNICATIONS

Spousal

Common wisdom claims spouses cannot be compelled to testify against each other. This is not strictly true, as shrewd investigators quickly discover. True enough, spouses cannot be compelled to testify about private conversations, but the court can make them testify about what they saw. In other words, if a husband comes bouncing into the kitchen and says, "Honey, I just robbed the bank," the wife cannot be compelled to testify to that conversation. But if she is driving by the bank and observes him dashing out with a gun and little canvas bag that she later sees at home full of money, she can be compelled to testify about that.

Whether this testimony is honest, factual, and accurate is another matter entirely. Investigators always interview spouses, but what they say is usually viewed as for background only unless it can be corroborated by other evidence or witnesses.

Attorney-Client

Other than the extremely rare instance when a client tells his attorney about a crime he intends to commit, attorneys cannot be compelled to testify against a client. For example, if a client tells his attorney that he intends to murder a key witness, the attorney is obligated to reveal this fact to the court. Otherwise attorney-client communications are the most privileged in the industry.

Investigator/Attorney-Client

Private investigators hired by attorneys to work on cases for their clients are also covered by this attorney-client privilege. In other words, I cannot be forced to tell what a client told me or how I got a piece of information when I work for a client through his attorney. Seems like those of us in this business get to test this concept at least once a week.

Doctor-Patient

Conversations, findings, records, and lab results between a patient and his medical doctor have traditionally been seen as privileged, but this is changing rapidly. In at least one state, a diagnosis of AIDS is now a matter of public record. Doctors can voluntarily testify on behalf of their client patients and often do, appearing as expert witnesses. As an aside, absolutely all medical records must be made part of any court proceeding involving personal injury.

ADMISSIBLE VS. INADMISSIBLE EVIDENCE

Exhibits—including photography, newspaper articles, letters, computer disks, sketches, diagrams, and statements—that have a bearing on the case are generally admissible as evidence. Whether it is helpful or wise to attempt to admit this evidence is up to the attorney handling the case. All exhibits must be labeled and dated.

Illegally seized evidence cannot be introduced into court as evidence. This is often a very productive field of research for private investigators. If they are able to prove evidence was improperly acquired and the evidence is material to the proceedings, the opposition's entire case might collapse. On the other hand, expect the other side to try mightily to impeach any key evidence you turn up in support of your client as being illegally acquired.

Investigators—even older, experienced ones—are notorious for bringing evidence to their attorney that is completely inadmissible. However, it is not worthless because it says something about the case and the people involved, but it cannot be used in court. For example, recently I discovered that a 13-year-old girl alleging statutory rape had a raging case of venereal disease, whereas the accused was as clean as driven snow. In another case, a a 15-year-old material witness to a murder worked as a prostitute in a large neighboring city. Both sets of facts were interesting but completely inadmissible, I was quickly informed.

These are only the basic rules of evidence for criminal and civil cases as they relate to private investigators. Rules of evidence are often obscure, mysterious, and frustrating. The only way to work around them is to keep in close contact with the lead attorney. Usually all this is decided on a case-by-case basis, after long and arduous consultation of state law books.

TIPS FOR POTENTIAL WITNESSES

1. If you are charged with a crime and must depend on a public defender, you should be prepared to argue your own case. Public defenders are notorious for being unprepared.
2. Spousal privilege is not complete. You can be compelled in certain circumstances to testify against a spouse, though communications between spouses are generally exempt.
3. Communications between you and your doctor may not be protected. Find out the laws in your state to be sure
4. Find out what the law is in your state for submitting to a recorded interview.
5. Be sure any evidence used against you is legally obtained. If possible, think of reasons why evidence should be disallowed when dealing with your opponents.

5

CRIMINAL INVESTIGATIONS

SHOOTING TWO WHITETAILS WOULDN'T HAVE been so bad, except that it was done from a busy highway; it occurred after season's end; it involved exceptional trophy-class critters with massive, valuable horns; and the skin and meat were left out in the open to rot. All the two carpenters who killed the deer took were the horns, head, and cape. Big mistake! Hoisting a few rounds at the Brass Rail before heading out for the hunt destroyed any caution the two buddies might ordinarily have used.

With such evidence in plain view, it was not long before the finger of suspicion pointed in the direction of the two carpenters. Officials of fish and game departments realize that dead animals can't talk about how they arrived in that condition and that other human witnesses who can talk are seldom available. Perhaps for this reason, of all law enforcement types, some of the best, most highly trained and practiced criminal interrogators work state fish and game cases. These may be local or county cops, but they don't send out amateurs on these sorts of cases! Such was true in this case as well. The top-drawer authorities, geared up for one of their periodic antipoaching campaigns, reacted quickly to this case, probably probably as a result of an anonymous tip from a passing motorist using a cell phone. Maybe it was boastful talk at the bar, but we never figured out for sure how the wardens were put on to my clients so quickly.

Each unsuspecting carpenter was at his home when a law enforcement team descended almost simultaneously at each place. At most, only a half mile separated the homes of the two, leaving no time or opportunity for the poachers to synchronize their stories. Each law enforcement team was prepared to "explain" to its subject that it had a signed confession from the other guy, "So you might as well give us your version of what happened." The investigators spent most of the day at one fellow's house. Police interrogations can go on for 10 or 12 hours, but this was a "voluntary" conversation. No warrant was in effect, neither man was under detention, and it was arguable whether they were "in interrogation." Miranda rights (or the right to have an attorney present and the right to remain silent to avoid self-incrimination) did not apply. It may not have looked like it at the time, but these follows were cleverly manipulated into "voluntary" cooperation.

Police interrogators were so successful that within two hours they had one of the men virtually crawling on the floor, hopelessly and shamelessly spilling his guts. The other fellow refused to talk to the authorities. His silence may have saved his behind in the short run, but his accomplice's confession eventually got him too.

The two golden rules of police (criminal) interrogation are as follows: (1) absolutely nothing said by police interrogators will be the truth; and (2) effective police interrogators always have a well-thought-through, time-proven plan in mind before starting to work on any suspect. There is nothing different between the techniques of private investigators and those used by the police except for the incredible lengths to which criminal investigators will go to come up with pretexts. In hindsight, these pretexts often defy imagination.

In the deer-poaching case, interrogators assured the one poacher who agreed to talk that:

1. They had a positive identification on both men. There were several eyewitnesses who were driving by in their vehicles and saw the two shoot the deer. Since these eyewitnesses were animal rights' advocates who hated deer hunters, they were willing to do whatever they could to ensure that the men were punished. Even now, these witnesses were at the sheriff's office signing their statements.
2. They had a signed confession from the other poacher.
3. After getting a search warrant for the poachers' houses and garages, they could easily match the DNA from the deer head, horns, and cape found in the possession of the poachers with the carcasses left out in the field. All of this was, of course, a complete fabrication.

Witnesses are often confused and uncertain about details. Should there actually have been eyewitnesses in the poaching case (which there weren't), investigators *might* have been able to demonstrate that they saw one of the men (they couldn't know which for sure) shoot *at* the deer. The search warrant bluff was another relatively easy matter. If the fellow hadn't voluntarily surrendered the trophy, police investigators would have had to drive all the way to the courthouse and convince a reluctant judge to issue a search warrant. By that time the fellow and the head could have been a hundred miles away. But within a short time, law enforcement officials had a signed confession, "voluntarily" provided, incriminating both men.

Private investigators frequently run into situations where their clients have been lied to by police. The following examples are commonly heard from clients:

- "They told me a neighbor happened to look out of the window and could positively identify me."
- "They had my fingerprints from the doorknob, plaster casts of my truck tracks, my footprints, phone taps, and even videos from the ATM across the street of me forcing the girl."

Not only will good police interrogators lie about witnesses, they will lie to discredit an alibi.

- "The DEA took pictures of me from a hang glider making a drug sale out in the county, conclusively proving that my alibi was phony."
- "They told me that if I was really walking down Third Street that night as I said I was, I would have seen the broken city water main."

Ethical private investigators are troubled by these dishonest tactics. Even if a suspect is a scumbag, his story should be checked out—it might be true. Our judicial system was designed to give the benefit of the doubt to the accused.

In all fairness, police interrogators sometimes do a cursory alibi check if they have the manpower and it is convenient. Otherwise they will use pretexts to break an alibi as quickly and economically as possible. Some suspects have been intentionally, almost forcibly led down the primrose path. Who of us can recall exactly what we did three or even two nights ago, in the face of a smooth-talking, uniformed interrogator who is accusing us of a very serious offense?

Criminal interrogators use small, stark, simple rooms containing only two chairs that they position 3 to 4 feet apart, if they can get you to agree to such. Folks thus maneuvered should scream for their lawyer but often don't. Private investigators refer to this lapse as "felony stupid." People dumb enough to commit felonies generally don't think things through. They don't have money for attorneys, and they often voluntarily subject themselves to this almost irresistible challenge because they really believe they are clever enough to lie their way out of their predicament. However, they usually cannot withstand clever interrogators. I have actually encountered innocent parties with valid, air-tight alibis who confessed to crimes in front of especially motivated police interrogators.

Private investigators can usually detect clients who have had numerous scrapes with the law. Veteran offenders will sit far away so an interrogator cannot get close enough to see their eyes or secretly record their statements. They will keep their answers short, limited to the specific question without providing any extra details. For example:

"Are you married?"
"Yes."
"To whom?"
"My wife."
"What is her name?"
"Maria."
"Is she from here?"
"No."
"How much do you contribute to her support?"
"A bundle."
"When did you see her last?"
"Can't recall."

Just a few months ago in a criminal case with which I am familiar, police interrogators tricked a victim into confessing by telling him the conversation wasn't being recorded. "You told me you weren't recording this conversation, and besides it's against this state's law to record without the knowledge and permission of both parties," the victim later complained.

"Yes," the criminal interrogator admitted. "I lied and, besides, we use this tape to uncover leads, not for court-admissible evidence."

Recording without both parties' consent is illegal in many states—including the one in which this happened—but what is the victim going to do after the recording is made? Options are usually very limited—especially if the police investigators have already convinced the subject to plead guilty.

Along with providing elaborate but phony pretexts, police interrogators will also put on their friendly "it's okay, it doesn't really matter, it isn't a serious crime" face. In the case of the beleaguered deer poachers, the investigators took along one of the county's best-known, most gregarious officers. The investigators started their "voluntary" conversation with absolute trivia. The one naive carpenter assumed that if he refused to talk, it would prove that he was guilty as alleged.

As crazy as it sounds, the fellow who confessed assumed that because he knew the officer, who was acting friendly, it was okay for him to talk about what happened. Slowly, surely the skilled interrogator drew the fellow into the trap. As mentioned, good investigators go to great lengths to give subjects good cause to tell all they know. In the case of the two deer poachers, the officers stressed that everything was understandable and not really a problem. "These were very old deer, white with age, and the meat left behind would have been tough as old wang leather," one officer assured them. "The meat would not have been edible anyway because of where the deer were shot," the two shooters were told over and over. The investigators knew all the while that the poachers' eyesight, fuzzy from drinking, was not keen at the time of the shooting so they wouldn't know how old the deer were or where they were shot. Plus, they knew that the deer had been shot through the front quarters, ruining only 30 percent of the meat.

Theirs was an excellent plan. Once the one poacher became ensnared, escape was difficult, if not impossible, for the two. In hindsight, their best recourse would have been to refuse to talk at all. Amen. Period. I know it's repetitious, but please recall that good investigators or interrogators always find a pretext to get you to talk.

Do police interrogators still use the good-cop/bad-cop routine? Although some police departments undoubtedly still use it, the friendly pretext-laden routine we see today is far more common because it is so successful.

Criminal cases are not the bread-and-butter of most attorneys. Again, contrary to impressions from TV, attorneys do not generally specialize in criminal law because very few criminals have funds for lawyers' fees. Using private investigators is a cheaper, easier, more thorough method of handling criminal cases for many attorneys. In small part, increased use of private investigators may result from this fact. It's cheaper to use investigators, and attorneys don't like criminal cases to begin with.

Reviewing quickly:

1. Those even remotely suspected of specific criminal activities will be questioned for hour after hour—if allowed—by skilled, trained, practiced police interrogators. Initially, these officers will appear friendly and even benign to the subject. Coffee, snacks, rest room breaks, and soothing words will be used to reinforce this "friendship."
2. Civil and criminal interviews are similar in that good investigators will devise clever pretexts to induce subjects to talk. In the case of criminal investigations, these pretexts will be extremely clever and may even have two

or three parts to them. Some are absolutely unbeatable. One attorney reported an instance where a young woman was told that her mother was in the hospital in critical condition as a result of a car collision and that the daughter should finish the interview so she could be at her mother's side when she died.

3. Pretexts often allege evidence or witnesses that are entirely fictional, including very clever ruses that cast doubt on alibis. Even very honest people begin to wonder whether they could they be dreaming!

4. Since most of us really don't like being in trouble with "the Law," police investigators will give suspects some understandable reason why they did the ugly deed as well as someone on whom to blame the crime other than themselves. In many cases, the scapegoat is the victim himself. For example, interrogators will often say something like, "He was a rich bastard with a Mercedes and a cell phone, so taking a few dollars from his loan shark business was his own fault, not yours, wasn't it?"

5. All investigators modify and tailor their speech to fit the subject. They avoid harsh, incriminating sentences or even words. Rather than using the word *shoplifted*, they will use *boosted* or *borrowed*. Rather than *armed robbery*, they refer to *a job* or *the convenience store.* Rape will be *a poke*. Normally rough-talking police are extremely cautious at this point in the process.

Private and criminal investigators are the same in this regard. For example, during the course of my work I often interview people in jail or in "the joint." Customarily, written statements given by these badasses to corrections officers are packed full of profanities and invective. I treat the convicts with whom I speak with respect and never use profanity. They respond in kind, often giving me really good information others have missed, overlooked, or dismissed as untruthful.

Convicts are typically lying scumbags, but occasionally they give up a pearl.

6. After having confessed, most people dragged through this procedure by skilled police interrogators will take the next step and sign or even write out a complete confession. Oral confessions have often been used in court successfully but aren't as effective as written confessions. As we will see from examples cited in this book, overcoming a written confession is really tough.

7. Suspects (and their attorneys and investigators) can't count on police officers *not* getting the Miranda rights down correctly and their being released on a technicality. Mirandizing suspects is old hat to officers now and no longer an inconvenience. I cannot recall a successful challenge to Mirandarization!

All this, melded together with the other information in this book on interviewing witnesses and using pretexts, is how it works in the police shop.

TIPS FOR POTENTIAL WITNESSES

1. Believe nothing you are told by investigators.
2. Do not allow yourself to be interviewed without your attorney being present.
3. The only defense is not to talk *at all*. As we keep saying, it's like the first bite of peanuts—police investigators know that if they can get you started you will probably end up telling everything. Officers will tell you that if you refuse to talk you will be presumed guilty. They will tell you that they wouldn't be wasting their valuable time interviewing you if they didn't already assume you were guilty. Nothing changes when you refuse to talk—except life is easier for your investigator and attorney.
4. Keep your alibi very simple and straightforward, bereft of any details, *at least* until your attorney arrives.
5. Do not agree to the recording of your interrogation. Do everything you can to ensure that you're not being recorded illegally.
6. Always expect some sort of "you're not telling the truth because if you had been, blah, blah, blah, and you would have seen senn . . ."
7. We call it "felony dumb" in the trade: felons who honestly believe that they can talk their way out of a police interview. If you are guilty, don't talk to police interrogators at all.
8. Expect most attorneys not to handle criminal cases. This is because so few criminals have money for attorney fees.
9. Don't fall for the old line "It's OK—what you did is not so bad. If you confess, everything will be fine."

ONCE WITNESSES ARE IN THE LEGAL PIPELINE

THIS CHAPTER CONCENTRATES ON WITNESSES WHO, by one circumstance or another, are swept into the legal system, either willingly or unwillingly, and the role investigators play in the preparation of their testimony. It is often said, and will frequently be repeated, that a good attorney will never ask a question in court for which he does not already know the answer. It is the investigator's job to supply him with enough information so that he knows the answers. To do this, investigators may contact hundreds of potential witnesses in the almost blind hope that they will recall seeing someone or something. For example, I once contacted scores of factory workers to determine whether anyone saw someone walking along a certain road at 6:00 A.M. when their shift changed.

Witnesses who enter the legal pipeline are usually one of the following:

1. Criminals who have confessed or who cannot come up with a plausible alibi and then find themselves under indictment in court.

2. Civil defendants who have not mounted a vigorous enough defense and subsequently find themselves with their day in court scheduled.
3. Expert indirect and material witnesses whose observations, interpretations, and evaluations are judged to be of importance. The witness will know how important when an attorney calls or a subpoena arrives announcing the date the witness is to be deposed or to show up in court.

Once in the legal system, witnesses make the quantum leap from being the priority of investigators to being the wards of their attorneys. Casual witnesses, expert witnesses, and witnesses being deposed are handled similarly at this point. Investigators and attorneys having any brains, experience, common sense, desire to win, and responsibility to their clients will do the following:

- Research absolutely everything about a witness—background, family, biases, employment, income, honesty, and likely pattern of testimony.
- Make sure they know absolutely everything about the incident in question. The minuteness with which some of these key cases are investigated and reconstructed comes as a great shock to first-timers.
- Have a well-thought-out plan for talking to the witness. Using pretexts is unacceptable in court, but information you have already pried loose may be allowed in court and can be drawn out by a skillful trial lawyer.

EXPERT WITNESSES

If you end up in court as an expert witness (or prepare an expert witness for your side), expect that even in the most mundane cases, the opposition can and probably will find an expert to support its point of view. Judges and juries seem to expect and accept experts to disagree. When experts conflict, the case is settled on other issues. Dueling experts seem especially common in personal injury cases.

To help them find expert witnesses, good investigators and trial lawyers keep on file the names and qualifications of thousands of experts who can be contacted when needed for background information in their areas of expertise. For example, I am frequently called for information on homemade explosives and explosive devices. On the other hand, in my capacity as an investigator, within the past month I have interviewed other experts about the growth rate of hair, death by poisoning, herbicides, reconstructive surgery, timber regrowth rates, common farming techniques in our area, and teen drunkenness.

One quasi-expert in antiques tried to charge me for calling him, but generally the custom of the trade is to provide information free as long as the caller is paying the phone bill and no large block of the expert's time is required. Later these same cooperating experts may be retained to help defend or pursue a legal matter, but, as with most attorneys, the first visit is usually gratis.

A very few expert witnesses become so good at what they do that they achieve notoriety within the industry and are sometimes hired by one side or the other just to keep them off the other guy's team. But this situation is more rumored than actual. I know of only one man, an expert in public utilities matters, who fits this category, and he has a real winning combination. His specialty is so narrow that attorneys with well-heeled corporate clients quickly hire him the minute they even suspect their case *might* be one in which he could testify. He takes in tens of thousands of dollars per year in retainer fees, yet seldom actually testifies and hasn't even been deposed in many months.

Adding an expert's name to an official court witness list without his written permission or without paying him a retainer is completely unethical but surprisingly common.

Some attorneys do this to keep their client costs down while simultaneously trying to limit the experts available to the other side. They apparently believe that chances are good no one will notice, but I am currently involved in a disbarment action on this very issue.

Many experts are used over and over as witnesses, so they become good at court appearances, especially those in the wrongful injury circuit. There is a great difference between the testimony of an expert witness and that of an investigator. An expert can validly testify that, in his opinion, the subject will never work again, whereas I can only testify that I was the one who took the pictures of the fellow hanging drywall. Material witnesses, such as across-the-street neighbors, can testify that they saw the plaintiff pruning trees, whereas an expert witness can testify that it is possible for a person suffering from the plaintiff's specific disability to perform such a task, based on the expert's experience with such disabilities. Our modern legal system often produces two experts in the same court arguing entirely different conclusions. It is the job of the attorney to make his expert stand out by appearing more credible, trustworthy, sympathetic, or qualified. One way attorneys do this is by carefully choosing their expert's clothing. This may include having the expert wear his uniform with all his medals if he is a police officer or serviceman, or a nice, conservative suit and tie if the attorney wants him to blend in with the jury members. (Actually, dressing witnesses is a very precise field, but not one that we need to go into here since it is generally handled by the attorney, not the investigator.)

DEPOSITIONS

Depositions, for those new at this business, are a type of testimony under oath, where the person being deposed is asked to explain, often in great detail, what he saw, was told, heard, smelled, felt, or tasted. Testimony is limited to these areas, not to include what the witness guessed or assumed. Opinions are never allowed unless the witness is an expert in the area under consideration. Depositions are often done at the court recorder's office or in an attorney's office, but they can be held anywhere that is agreeable to all parties. All are recorded and transcribed at great expense to the litigants. Occasionally, they are done in the courthouse when one side or the other believes that a judge's intercession may be necessary.

Rules of engagement during depositions are different from those used in court when one testifies. Court rules tend to be complex. There is no point in going into the court rules here, since this book is limited to the role of investigators. Let the attorneys posture, object, and make motions, as well as advise you on how to proceed with your investigation.

RECOGNIZING AND DEALING WITH WITNESS BIAS

That very few witnesses are totally indifferent to a particular issue is often difficult for private investigators to understand. Investigators should expect witnesses to have biases when they interview them. Americans, by nature, like to take sides, rooting for their own team and against the opposition. Most people don't lie overtly. They selectively recall the part that supports their presupposition. Witnesses will color the circumstance to help what they perceive to be as their team. That's why some people won't say anything good about small-town merchants or anything bad about preachers.

Investigators should have a plan for dealing with witness bias before the interview takes place. All experienced investigators can cite numerous times when witnesses were reluctant to talk with them because they knew that to do so would assist those whom they perceived to be the opposition. Because of previous experience or disposition, they don't want to help if there is any way of avoiding it. An investigator's duty is not to change these people's team affiliation, but to find a reason for them to talk and express their own opinion. This is not always easy when the first question a witness asks is, "Who are you working for?" You should have a good pretext ready: "For myself. I am doing a story for the *National Enquirer*," I often claim. (No kidding, this has frequently worked for me. One time I even posed as a front man for a national TV syndicate doing a special show on the special situation a particular case presented.) Then the investigator can report to his client what the witness said and where he was coming from.

Under especially dicey circumstances (e.g., homicide cases), good investigators do not take the word of one person alone for anything because of the likelihood that the witness is biased. Corroboration by at least two others is vital. In a recent vehicular homicide case, I was hired by the defense to investigate the accident that resulted in the death. Basically, one vehicle, being driven by my client, struck a second vehicle, killing its driver. My client desperately needed some corroborating testimony about what really happened at the bloody intersection. A passenger in my client's vehicle reported seeing a car behind the victim's vehicle at the stop sign. Against all odds, I located two eyewitnesses, one earwitness, and two other drivers who came on the scene in their vehicles immediately after the accident. There was no need to use pretexts on these people; they were simply interested (and proud) to report what they thought they saw. They verified each other's accounts. No one reported another vehicle behind the victim's.

In the same case, the older brother of the accused was positive that the victim had illegally driven her car across a vacant lot and onto the street where she was struck by my client's vehicle. This scenario initially seemed credible because of the final resting places of the crashed vehicles. However, no witness could confirm that the victim roared across the empty lot, and a vehicle reconstruction expert adequately explained a different scenario of how both vehicles could have come to rest where they did down the avenue.

In this example, I did not take any one witness' word for anything. None of the people were lying overtly—they were simply supporting their team the best way they could. Investigators know that team spirit is very difficult to overcome. In another example, the entire crew of an Alaskan crab fishing vessel refused to believe that one of their members had committed an especially heinous act and were willing to say or do virtually anything in court, including perjuring themselves, in his support.

Assessing the Honesty of Unfavorable Witnesses

It is frequently just as important for an investigator to uncover a potential witness' moral integrity and intelligence as it is to find out how he will come down on a specific issue or what vital piece of information he might or might not have. Attorneys frequently ask me, "Is that person honest?" I don't know. Perhaps I have been snookered out of some good stuff by potential witnesses who deliberately gave the impression that they were either lying bastards or as dumb as a box of rocks. If they were acting, they sure did it well. In such cases, I recommend that they be dropped as potential witnesses, which may have been part of their plan all along.

When an investigator knows that a witness is honest but favors the other side, he may attempt to introduce bits and pieces of evidence contradicting what the witness believes to get him to change his mind. Or the investigator may not divulge the contradictory information and let his attorney use it during the trial to confuse and discredit the witness.

But there is great danger in this of what is called *cognitive dissonance*, where a witness confronted by strong evidence he doesn't want to believe will simply quit talking or thinking about the case because it has become too painful.

Another tactic frequently employed by attorneys involves calling the reluctant witness to the stand but directing him to answer simply "yes" or "no" to questions about what he saw— e.g., "Did you see the accused standing in the garage at 413 Elm on November 12 with two tires over his arms?"

An opposing attorney may attempt to interject witness bias into the proceedings, but these contests always seem to go to the best prepared.

Are Depositions or Investigators Best for Uncovering Witness Bias?

A relatively recent shift away from relying entirely on depositions to discover witness bias is occurring as we speak. In our modern times, well-prepared attorneys want their investigators to have any information on witness bias in hand well before deposition time. In addition, taking depositions is more costly than hiring an investigator. Using investigators is frequently seen as a cost-cutting measure for clients who can't afford depositions.

The whole point is that investigators expect witnesses to have biases, and their job is to get witnesses to expose them. Then investigators report to their clients about the witnesses' biases and honesty, as well as whether the witnesses are part of any team. Having investigators do this saves the client money and scares off the other side. As we have all heard, a strong offense is the best defense.

PREPARING WITNESSES FOR COURT

It is often assumed that one of the great dangers of using a neophyte witness is that he will talk too much when he is being deposed or testifying in court—e.g., that he will be asked the time and instead will give the history of watch-making. In actual practice, this is usually only a danger early in the case when investigators ply the witnesses with guile and pretexts. By the time the case gets to court the time for long, rambling, detailed questions and answers has long passed. Good courtroom attorneys gain their leverage with short, quick, almost choppy questions that require short, direct answers. If that fails to elicit answers, the attorney will invoke the judge to instruct the witness to answer the questions directly.

Slowly and certainly, good trial lawyers will draw witnesses into the case to a place where any untrue or contradictory statements are impossible to explain or justify. This is the forte of the 1 or 2 percent of attorneys who are excellent trial lawyers.

Even honest, well-intentioned witnesses can occasionally be made to look dishonest or stupid in court. One might hope that this happens only to witnesses so blinded by their own prejudices or desire for a client's dollar that they cannot tell the simple truth, but it frequently happens even to expert witnesses. There are experts who make a good living testifying for the side that pays best. Within the industry they are known as "expert whores." These folks should expect intense cross-examination of their testimony.

Generally, investigators don't try to openly impeach witnesses with whom they talk. It is the investigator's duty to extract information for attorneys to use at a more auspicious time for impeachment purpose. If a subject is lying or even shading the truth, and the investigator figures out how an attorney can show this during the deposition or trial, the subject should count on being made to look like a lying fool.

Using Mock Cross-Examinations

Before tossing a witness into into the legal snake pit as a material witness, an expert witness, or a person being deposed, I recommend that he undergo at least five hours of rigorous mock cross-examination. This exposure is vital, especially for amateur testifiers who are unfamiliar with the ordeal that lies ahead. Usually young attorneys of varying experience undertake this chore.

On the other side, prosecuting attorneys seldom have the time or manpower for this type of exercise. They tend to assume that the police officers they primarily use have enough experience and know-how to stay out of trouble in court. But cops are notorious for not knowing when to stop talking, often jeopardizing the prosecutor's case.

Private parties to litigation, including civil cases, often do not wish to pay $200 to $300 per hour for practice sessions. They assume that the expert witnesses they hire will know what they are doing. This assumption can lead to disaster. Experts will be grilled about their qualifications in court. So not only are investigators expected to find needed experts, but they are to verify and document the experts' qualifications for their client.

Do Your Homework

When preparing witnesses for court (or yourself if you are being called as the investigator), assume that the other side has done its homework and has in its possession letters, videos, newspaper quotes, taped statements, historic data, criminal records, notes, and especially sworn statements taken during deposition. Surprising numbers of witnesses forget what they said when being deposed regarding obscure evidence. I once worked a case that could have turned on a lone, four-line note my client wrote, never sent, and then reportedly lost. Up till the end I turned over heaven and earth to be sure the note was not in the opposition's hand.

Being proven in court to be a liar or hopelessly biased is extremely embarrassing. Every investigator has his own examples. These are three of mine:

- A 13-year-old girl alleged that she had consensual sex with an adult, which, given their ages, constituted statutory rape. She claimed that the first incident occurred along a riverbank in broad daylight on a day that official weather records indicated was in the 30s with cold, misting rain. Would she likely expose herself in such weather? The jury thought not.
- A middle-aged man alleged total disability as a result of lung damage from working 25 years in a sawmill. A photograph taken from a neighbor's window clearly showed him using a chain saw to cut down and then cut up a large, tall tree. On the basis of the photo, the jury decided that he was a shameless malingerer.
- A homeowner who employed casual day labor to help construct his new home was totally devastated when one of the men filed a complaint against him about an alleged workplace accident. An in-depth record search uncovered evidence of similar claims in the recent past by the plaintiff against other naive property owners. A jury assumed the plaintiff was lying about his injuries.

WHAT TO TAKE TO COURT WITH YOU

Be aware that any records, crib sheets, or written aids taken into court by a witness can and probably will become part of the public record. I have never seen it personally, but a fellow investigator recalls the time a Public Utilities Commission employee took an entire office file, including confidential cost structure analyses, into court. All this material ended up as part of the public record, causing great embarrassment and discomfort for the employee.

If there is the possibility that you might not be able to recall under courtroom duress the detailed observations you made about a case, it may be wise to rethink the honesty of your testimony. If your notes involve complex computations or facts the other side already has, it may not matter if the other team gets them. The main thing is to not carry anything into the courtroom that you do not want the other side to have access to.

TIPS FOR POTENTIAL WITNESSES

1. If you hire a private investigator to help a family member, you should let the investigator work on ways of getting him out of trouble, not on being a good conversationalist or hearing your confessions. You'd be amazed at the money people waste just chitchatting to private investigators.
2. If you don't want to testify, consider trying to leave the impression with the investigator that you are either lying or too dumb to answer the questions accurately.
3. If you are a witness and an investigator shows up, expect that he will

   - be surprised and doubtful if you have no built-in biases
   - employ a strong pretext to get you to expose those biases, along with everything else you know about the case
   - tactfully, quietly probe the weaknesses in your biases
   - evaluate your honesty and intelligence and report these to his client

4. Realize that the one piece of information that could cast doubt on your entire testimony may be in the investigator's hands.
5. Expect that witnesses will disagree. Don't be

surprised when the other team has an expert who disagrees with your testimony.

6. If you are truly reluctant to testify for one reason or another, hide this reluctance carefully from the investigator. The rule is—don't set yourself up to be a target by overtly, stubbornly refusing to testify. Investigators can (and will) destroy targets when they set their mind to it.

7. If you feel that you *cannot* appear, I recommend that you just disappear. This ain't the movies. The number of absolutely key witnesses is very small. Almost all cases are won using one key point with lots of smaller corroborating points. However, if your testimony is absolutely vital, running won't help anyway. You will still be found, perhaps poorer and more beleaguered.

8. Amateurs—even those who have read this book—are advised to "cooperate cautiously" with the investigation at first, at least until they have more experience with the system.

9. If you have to testify in court and you don't want to answer certain questions directly, you could try to ramble or answer the question with a question. If successful, this might foil the attorney's cleverly devised plan of attack and throw him off. Be aware, however, that the judge may instruct you to answer the question in a direct manner. Also be aware that this isn't a tactic for those inexperienced with the system.

10. If you are asked a convoluted question with numerous subsets and digressions, ask the attorney to repeat the question, giving you time to think about your answer. Or ask that the question be repeated one point at a time. The fact

that you apparently cannot decipher the question sends a message to the jury that the attorney is deliberately trying to confuse you.

11. Never attempt to lie in court about anything significant or detailed. Assume that the other side has done its homework and has in its possession letters, videos, newspaper quotes, taped statements, historic data, criminal records, or notes about you, as well as your sworn statements. A surprising number of witnesses forget what they said about obscure evidence when they were deposed.

SURVIVING A CROSS-EXAMINATION

(Unlike other chapters in this book written from the perspective of the investigator, this chapter is written from the viewpoint of the witness who is facing cross-examination. It tells regular people which tactics and techniques will likely be used by top attorneys in their cross-examinations and how to survive them.)

CROSS-EXAMINATION OF WITNESSES IS THE ONE defining area of trial law where the sheep are separated from the goats. It's strictly lawyer's play, with the investigator confined to the sideline as advisor.

Outsiders who don't really know what is going on often find courtroom drama fascinating—as long as they are observers and not players. This chapter may not teach you how to enjoy being cross-examined in court, but it will show you how to survive it.

Legally, testimony in court goes as follows:

1. *Direct testimony*. Prompted by questions from the attorney who called you, during direct testimony you tell your version of events. This is also where previously sworn testimony, given in deposition, is read into the court record.
2. *Cross-examination*. After an attorney has allowed you to present your version of the story to the judge and jury, he is obligated by procedural rules to turn you over to the opposing side to answer its questions.
3. *Redirect testimony*. After your cross-examination, your attorney has the opportunity to repair any damage through redirect testimony. Just be aware that a shrewd cross-examiner can often do so much damage to the witness, or inflict the damage in such a subtle way, that an attorney cannot rehabilitate his witness through redirect.

If it's a high-profile trial or the other side wants to win very badly, by the time you take the stand the cross-examining attorneys will have been fully briefed by their investigators all about you—your family history (e.g., you spoke French at home and went to Quebec as a Mormon missionary), your natural biases regarding this case, your financial situation, your employment history, and your hobbies. The cross-examiner will blend these together to form a plan virtually guaranteed to include some very difficult questions, especially if you are using questionable evidence to support an unrealistic position.

Broad brushes often paint foolishly wide, but in most instances, good trial lawyers start their cross-examinations by being exceptionally nice to you. They know that even experienced witnesses are apprehensive, and ordinary witnesses tend to be really scared. Like cops in criminal cases or the investigator who first talked to you, an experienced lawyer will attempt to get you to like and trust him and then lull you into complacency while slowly, steadily leading you into contradictory, compromising, and ambiguous statements. The attorney will usually begin by asking simple questions about family or personal trivia.

"You were born in a hospital in River City?"

"Your mother and father went to high school here?"

"You have three younger brothers?"

"You are currently working at the Holiday Inn as a maintenance man?"

"You have never taken anything from your employer?"

Note that, once the process starts, you will be fed questions that you generally confirm with a simple "yes" or "no." It has already been noted that attorneys never ask questions to which they don't already know the answer. This is not always true, but it is a pretty good working principle. As do investigators, trial lawyers will avoid certain harsh words such as *murder, rape, steal,* or *child molester* until they are ready to make a sometimes harsh point later in the case. Instead, you will get a couple of carefully planned slow balls that can easily be hit out of the park. "Oh," you say to yourself, "I have the upper hand with this guy, who is neither as bright nor as hostile as I had first supposed."

Attorneys who are good at cross-examinations are breathtakingly good. Using tiny steps, they slowly, carefully lead both expert and material witnesses into certain destruction. Am I being cynical? I think not. I have often asked attorneys whether it is the case and the evidence or the pleadings that carry the day. Good evidence, they admit, is helpful, but in three out of five cases it's how the evidence is presented that makes the difference—especially during cross-examination.

Fine trial lawyers have a prodigious ability to absorb facts in a logical, orderly sequence. Then when they are on their feet and you are in the witness chair, it seems as though they can think "on their feet" faster than anyone else in the courtroom. Regrettably, this often includes opposing counsel. For instance, a trial lawyer in cross-examination will seemingly not notice or slide right past a glaring inconsistency or error on your part. Even the opposing attorney may conclude that the point was missed. But on summation, when it is no longer possible for the other side to clarify or explain, the patient attorney will bring out this inconsistency with devastating impact.

"Ladies and gentlemen of the jury," the attorney will say, "I would like to point out a strange and wonderful anomaly. On the one hand, Mr. Witness says this, but on the other he claimed something entirely different . . ." All you can do is twist in the wind.

LEARN THE POINTS OF LAW

What should you do when you learn that you will have to testify and undergo cross-examination? If there is no time or money for a mock cross-examination, at the very least you should find out the exact point or points of law that govern the case. It has been my experience that some mediocre trial lawyers don't even know this themselves, much less explain it to their clients or witnesses, but good trial lawyers will know exactly what legal theory they are attempting to apply. Don't go into court uninformed and legally unprepared. It's one of the cardinal rules for witnesses.

IMPEACHING WITNESSES

Two methods are available to attorneys to impeach a witness. Either your integrity can be attacked—including your character, background, bias, and experience (if you're an expert witness)—or the evidence and its conclusion itself can be discredited. Attacking the character of a witness is inadvisable without good, solid evidence. Investigators look for past news stories, statements to friends and family, letters, e-mails, court records, club memberships, and anything else that may reflect on you for use by the attorney. If you have a criminal record, be aware that it may also be revealed in court. Good attorneys always try to get a witness' past indiscretions admitted into the record.

- "You say you observed the witness sitting in the car with the victim? How did you know it was the victim? By what exact means did you positively identify the two of them?"
- "Have you ever been involved in a case of mistaken identity?"

The first approach questions the evidence as you thought you saw it; the other questions your past record and general integrity.

EXPERT WITNESSES

Expert witnesses should expect questions and statements on cross-examination that document, authenticate, or question their expertise. For example: "Dr. Smith, you are familiar with such and such a type medical condition, and this type of condition is documented in such and such a medical reference book, which you coauthored. Is that correct?" If you answer yes, expect more detailed questions about the last time you actually saw a real-life case of this exact type in person, how often you see such cases, and how the medical condition before the court applies to those you have experienced. Expect any limits or drawbacks to your current experience or knowledge to be probed thoroughly by the cross-examiner. Effective trial lawyers will know practically as much about the condition they are litigating as the expert on the stand! One attorney I knew, for instance, knew more about *E-coli* food poisoning than any medical doctor in the state and perhaps in the nation.

QUESTIONS OF YOUR CHARACTER

"Are you into flying saucers, men from Mars secretly hidden away in a hangar in Arizona by our government, crystals, channeling, or Trilateral Commission conspiracies?" Although casting doubt on your overall testimony by exposing offbeat beliefs can backfire, under certain circumstances some attorneys may use this approach successfully. A great deal depends on the circumstances of the case. If that's all the attorney has, he may use it. If you once did something as a result of hearing voices, expect to be gently and expertly led in that direction during cross-examination. Upon getting an admission that you have heard (or do hear) voices, skillful trial lawyers will usually drop the subject until they summarize, and then it will come back with a roar.

Generally, most cross-examiners will steer clear of actually slinging mud at your character. There is too much chance that the jury will take your side or the judge will rule that the evidence is improperly applied or inappropriate.

GETTING TO THE TRUTH

How can you determine whether the cross-examiner believes you are either lying or heavily shading facts to fit your presuppositions? One not-too-subtle device is to ask you to repeat your testimony over and over in great detail. What seems like senseless repetition really isn't. The cross-examiner hopes that ambiguities and inconsistencies will surface in your testimony. However, this tactic is not nearly as effective as it once was and now is generally used only by amateur cross-examiners. Modern juries quickly tire of the repetition, as do judges. In fact, less than a year ago, the judge in a very high-profile trial near where I live, repeatedly told the defense to move on and to stop haranguing the witness. The rule is about three hours for a cross-examination of a witness before boredom and inattention set in. Additionally, small ambiguities may actually legitimize your testimony in some jurors' minds because it doesn't sound rehearsed.

Another common—and much more effective—tactic is for the cross-examiner to have you start in the middle of your story and go forward and backward as he directs. The theory is that if he can get away from the logical order, you will be more truthful.

"You opened the door, only to experience a dense cloud of smoke pouring out of the room," the attorney says.

"No," you reply, carefully but minimally correcting his obviously leading question. "I opened the door and saw the cat sitting on the sofa; there was little smoke."

The rule is that if you are suspected of not telling the whole truth or of shading the truth, you will *not* be allowed to tell your story in logical sequence.

The successful use of this tactic requires that the examining attorney have a very clear, logical mind capable of absorbing great detail. Effective cross-examiners do not have to be orators if they have street sense and are logical. As mentioned, few attorneys have this ability to keep everything straight, so you probably don't have to worry about facing this tactic in your cross-examination.

THE START-AND-STOP TACTIC

Cross-examiners will continually stop and start testimony, leading to great digressions and false starts. This is primarily used for material witnesses, but you may experience something similar if you are an expert witness. It happened to me recently.

"You say that explosives allegedly used by the defendant would have had to have been expertly placed within the building to do the damage we see, but we just heard that the defendant was in the parking lot at the time. How short a delay between placement and detonation is possible in such a situation? Please start by telling us about readying the charge for detonation." Here the attorney used a herky-jerky start-and-stop series of questions calculated to throw me off balance and destroy my credibility.

If you don't have a clear idea of what happened or how the evidence suggested it happened or you are tying to bluff your way through, you can get thoroughly confused by this tactic. As Mark Twain said, "If you tell the truth, you don't have to remember anything."

DON'T EXPECT BROAD QUESTIONS

Experienced cross-examiners do not throw out broad questions that allow you to ramble or, more important, to qualify previous answers you may have handled poorly. Again, they seldom ask questions to which they do not already know the answer.

You will probably make some honest mistakes that can be cleared up during redirect. Trial lawyers, juries, and judges are tolerant of some of this.

As in basic investigators' interviews, lots of really good information comes after the attorney finally says, "Nothing more." That's the time you are relaxed and relieved that the ordeal is over. The trial lawyer will shout out one last question—often of critical importance—as you are about to leave the witness chair. Your best tactic is to ignore the question unless directed by the judge to answer or it has obvious potential to erroneously bias the jury. Attorneys must carefully choreograph such last-minute ambushes, but, just as investigators try to catch their subject off-guard at the end of interviews, so do attorneys. It happens often enough to warrant this cautionary note. Always remember that it ain't over till the fat lady sings—or you are safely out in the hall.

DOWN-AND-DIRTY TACTICS

Some attorneys use down-and-dirty questions that have no real purpose other than degrading you personally. Good trial lawyers won't use these tactics because they know that juries usually aren't impressed with these antics. In one trial, an admittedly overpursued (for the considerable assets that he had skillfully hidden) ex-husband was hounded mercilessly by his ex-wife, who was looking for assets to grab in response. He directed his investigator to find absolutely all of the dirt on her possible (there was quite a bit) and then ordered his attorney to bring it all out in court. The attorneys got an extra day or two of billable time, but I figured the jury was becoming so sympathetic to the ex-wife as a result of all this dirt that they may have been inclined to side with her even though we were actually proving she was a real witch.

Again, like everything in this business, you must learn to keep your eye on the ball. If you didn't say anything important during your direct testimony, you may not be cross-examined. Good attorneys who perceive that no real damage was done by what you said often shock everyone into silence by simply saying, "No questions." Facing an attorney who knows when to shut up—or not to speak at all—can be devastating for you, the witness. Only real experts use it well. When it occurs, your first reaction is that you have been given a reprieve. Obviously, this is a dramatic oversimplification.

COMPROMISING AND CONTRADICTORY QUESTIONS

Experienced trial lawyers learn to disguise their shock and anger while simultaneously leading you into losing your temper. When circumstances warrant it, expect a good trial lawyer to attempt to really anger you.

Witnesses, both material and expert, are often asked what they suspect may be a very compromising question.

This question may allude to a letter, taped interview, newspaper article, or other piece of information that involves you, which—if presented in evidence—can completely destroy your position and standing as a witness. In times past it may have been obscure letters, perhaps sent months before the issue became apparent. Letters are no longer much of an issue in our culture, but taped phone conversations, TV interviews, or e-mail messages certainly are.

The golden rule of modern witness cross-examination is that if something is out there to contradict your current testimony, and it's alluded to in cross-examination, you may well end up reading it for the court. Your testimony will be substantially destroyed.

When I am to be cross-examined, I *always* assume the other side has this stuff. That's what investigators are paid to dig up. An investigator quoted in the *Wall Street Journal* cautioned that key players in our society should expect to face any statements they have ever made either in writing or while being interviewed. That is good, practical advice in our modern society.

Whatever else, keep in mind that cross-examiners are extremely clever at orchestrating the sequence of questions to achieve their objectives. These objectives may include making you look foolish, dishonest, stupid, or uncertain. As mentioned, this will probably be accomplished by initially putting you at ease, making you comfortable, and then leading you on little by little. Forthrightness or fairness is usually not part of the formula.

Another rule of cross-examination is that trial lawyers will work hard at getting you into areas of the case that you are unprepared for and that you have not thought through. Modern investigators have made this process quite a bit easier for attorneys doing cross-examinations because they can provide attorneys with lots of material to work with.

Witnesses of all kinds are usually not accustomed to

dealing with issues that are not entirely black and white. Good attorneys are. They claim that effective cross-examinations are usually a collection of little probables rather than one great telling point that wins the whole thing. "He who makes the fewest errors last usually wins the case" is the plaintive cry of attorneys.

• • •

I am frequently asked if there is a future for really sharp, well-done, effective cross-examinations. It's a good question in this age of virtually infallible scientific analysis. There is the general impression that we don't need to probe the witness' honesty when modern forensics can match fibers, identify body fluids, analyze chemicals, make ballistic matches, use lasers to detect fingerprints, and the Lord only knows what else to verify the truth of a matter.

Because of modern forensics we may no longer have to endure lengthy testimony from dubious handwriting experts, tire and track experts, and even eyewitnesses—or at least not as often. Extremely sophisticated computer-driven fiber analysis, for instance, along with unheard-of storage and retrieval capabilities, can now fix a suspect at the scene of a crime or establish responsibility in civil actions. This may explain the oft-lamented demise of really good cross-examining trial lawyers, but records from before the turn of the century indicate there weren't many top trial lawyers then either!

My opinion is that, in some instances, modern scientific analysis has reduced the need for lengthy cross-examination. Investigators with all of their modern devices—including data banks, expert witness files, and the ability to retrieve documents from afar through fax machines—have scared off really bad actors. Totally biased witnesses have little chance of surviving in the modern courtroom.

The need for sharp, intelligent cross-examination is still

there, but it will be tempered and improved by modern investigation, both on the ground and in the laboratory. Cross-examinations now are much shorter and more intense.

So the answer is a definite maybe!

Could I withstand a top-notch cross-examination given what I know about the process? The answer is a definite "no" if I were required to lie about the event. I would quickly be made to look like a lying fool or worse. Remember that if *you* are ever facing cross-examination.

MILITARY
INTERROGATIONS

THE DIFFERENCE BETWEEN INTERROGATION and questioning is often the level of coercion involved. Military interrogation obviously involves significant coercion, whereas the mostly volunteer questioning I am engaged in requires little.

Sometimes the lines are blurred. Whenever a witness with whom I really need to discuss an issue stonewalls me, I don't hesitate to remind him that it isn't much trouble to depose him, as judges and attorneys are most cooperative in these circumstances. The cost to my client will rise $600 to $800, but, as I point out, he (the target of the investigation) will end up cooling his heels two or perhaps three days on this part alone. Even people with nothing to do don't want to waste three days of their time, especially when they realize the end result is the same as having spent 15 minutes talking to me when I originally asked them to.

It isn't the military, but it certainly is a form of coercion.

For information in this chapter I am indebted to my daughter, who went through military interrogators' school as part of her Arabic language training; my son, who is in the military; and Bill, a former Air

Most of us probably won't be involved as prisoners of war. Yet with our nation's heavy reliance on the National Guard—who knows? It never hurts to know the information in this chapter.

America helicopter pilot and military interrogator, who speaks fluent Vietnamese. In Bill's case, our extended conversations—while destroying significant supplies of Bulgarian red wine and perhaps some brain cells—led to my early understanding of modern military interrogation.

Let the record note, *military interrogation* is much different from *military intelligence,* which, according to my three experts, is an incredible oxymoron—on the same level as *real Naugahyde, jumbo shrimp,* or *honest politicians.*

Like everything else in this business, military interrogation is the same only different.

INTERROGATION TECHNIQUES: HONEY VS. VINEGAR

During Bill's era, reports frequently surfaced about Vietcong who were thrown out of helicopters or had their testicles toasted because of their resistance to interrogation. Many of these reports were probably accurate.

The use of torture in military interrogations is at worst the figment of fascist rabble and at best a third-rate method often having more adverse impact on interrogators in our culture than on the POWs being questioned. Those tortured will say whatever is necessary to get their tormentors to quit. Usually it's a hopeless mixing of truth and error that the interrogators and rear-echelon analysts who receive reports from the interrogators must try to make sense of.

To his great credit, even way back then before we really knew better, Bill insisted that torture was a completely foolish manner of dealing with POWs who had valuable information to impart. (Independent contemporary sources confirm this truth about Bill.) Bill doesn't recall such, but he may have been one of the originators of modern military interrogation, wherein the interrogator learns a great deal without beating up his subjects. Bill steadfastly maintains that the most he would do with a recalcitrant prisoner was to throw a bucket of cold water on him and sit him in front of an air conditioner. For most of these Vietnamese farm boys, it was their first experience with air conditioners and with being really cold!

"Think of what you are really trying to accomplish," Bill lectured as a kind of military version of keeping one's objectives firmly in sight. "If it's to win the war by quickly gathering as much information as possible while also encouraging scared, hungry, confused young soldiers to give in and talk, don't even think about coercive methods. It's what these soldiers are taught to expect. When the path ahead seems familiar, it is often difficult to extract information."

My son and daughter are of another era but are of the same mind regarding military interrogations. They both believe that the use of torture in military interrogations is counterproductive. "Think what would have happened in the Gulf War when thousands and thousands of prisoners streamed into our lines," my daughter said. "They were often told by their own officers that we would hurt them, but after days of unsupported cold, hungry misery in their own foxholes, they decided to risk it. They came in such tremendous numbers that incredible problems would have surfaced had not civility reigned on both sides."

The reluctance of the U.S. soldiers to hand over prisoners to interrogators probably started during the Korean conflict when, surprised and overwhelmed by human wave attacks, encircled GIs were frequently told to "take these POWs to the rear and be back in five minutes!" It was a sorry state of affairs from which many American participants, some of whom I know personally, never recovered psychologically.

Eventually the truth about the treatment of prisoners during the Korean conflict came out. The military prisoners were probably members of penal battalions controlled by the Chinese Communists. These penal battalions were made up of former Nationalist Kuomintang forces sent to the front lines as machine gun fodder. They had no small arms other than what they picked up and were not supported or resupplied by their own side. Certainly, all these prisoners wanted was to be left alone to go back to their families and farms.

(In their defense, U.S. Marines trapped up on the Chosen Reservoir were starving, freezing and cut off, and they figured that these prisoners were surrendering only to exhaust the Americans' limited supplies of food and clothing.)

It appears that this is the time Americans first started really evaluating not only the morality but also the effectiveness of roughing up prisoners. But even today U.S. field interrogators frequently report problems with front-line infantry who resent the nice treatment interrogators extend to POWs who may have just killed their buddies. Why treat prisoners so well, they wonder. It's like the cops who are nice to raping, stealing scuzzballs they generally hate and private investigators who engage in small talk while formulating a pretext to get their witnesses to spill their guts. It's called keeping your eyes on the prize. It's also the decent, human thing to do for people who have been captured.

Under the Geneva Conventions, POWs are obligated to provide only their name, rank, and serial number. My daughter recalls being taught that when prisoners were apprehended U.S. troops were obligated to immediately implement the "Rule of the Five S's":

1. Secure the POWs (i.e., make the captured troops "prisoners of war" in fact and deed).
2. Separate the POWs from the front and each other so stories can't be coordinated.
3. Sort the POWs into officers and enlisted men.
4. See to the safety of the POWs, including treatment of the wounded.
5. Supply food, water, and other sustenance to the POWs.

Like their civilian counterparts, military interrogators should focus on the main objective, which is finding out as much information as they can so they can win the war, quit killing each other, and all go home! Like private investigators, police interrogators, and courtroom cross-examiners, military interrogators are finally discovering that professionally ladled voluntary honey outperforms vengeful vinegar hands down in the information-gathering game.

DIFFERENCES BETWEEN CIVILIAN AND MILITARY INTERROGATIONS

There are some obvious differences between civilian and military interrogations. The most obvious difference is the ease or difficulty with which each can be avoided. Though it is not always true, conventional wisdom suggests that, unlike civilians, military subjects can't go into hiding and refuse to talk to investigators. Most of us assume that POWs are in compounds someplace and can be located pretty easily.

"They all receive tracking numbers, which should allow us to find them again," my daughter says, "but in real life, military witnesses often get lost in the shuffle." On the other hand, civilian witnesses usually can't hide as well as we assume they can, especially when investigators are determined to find them. In this regard, our customary thinking is incorrect about both military and civilian subjects.

Another difference between civilian and military interrogations is their results. Good private investigators *should* learn something from every witness with whom they speak, whereas good military interrogators *always* learn something from every one of their "customers." Military interrogators rely a great deal more than private investigators on what is brought in with the prisoner, the circumstances of his capture, and his physical condition.

For instance, during the reduction of Stalingrad, Russian General Zhukov reportedly told his interrogators to look for lice on starving, dirty German soldiers. When lice became epidemic among the captives, Zhukov knew the end was near, no matter what stout-hearted, hard-core, Nazi POWs claimed. For their part, German soldiers generally knew a big Russian offensive was imminent when they started encountering very young, raw recruits carrying brand-new weapons loaded with the latest production ammo.

During Desert Storm, Western forces knew instantly there was a serious problem when devout Iraqi Muslims were picked up in a seriously unwashed condition. Muslims pray at least once a day, and they do not pray unwashed. Going several days without prayer for these folks is so serious a breach that it cannot readily be contemplated by folks in our Western culture.

Although some military interviews are surprisingly similar to nonmilitary ones, there is at least one element that is markedly different: the half-life of military information is often dramatically shorter than that for information from a civilian setting. Accounts about who slipped on the ice, where, and how he fell may be useful for a long time, whereas the timeliness of information about the 49th Mechanized Rifles' being pulled out of the area yesterday to be sent to reinforce an area to the north is probably much more limited.

For example, during Desert Storm a group of dug-in Iraqis reported adequate supplies of food and water to their captors. But within four short days, these supplies could be used up, spoiled, stale, or inadequate. What would be the half-life of this type of information? What was true on modern battlefields a few hours ago may not be true right now. Dissemination of information in a timely manner is a critical problem of modern warfare. However, interrogators who simply report what they see and hear usually don't have to deal with the dissemination of the information they collect.

Civilian investigators like myself often have a problem getting around to all pertinent witnesses quickly and efficiently. In most adverse circumstances I figure I have about five hours before buzzing phone lines alert potential witnesses that I am on the ground and exactly what pretexts I am using. POWs can't avoid interrogators unless they choose honor and death over surrender, but on some days military interrogators must feel like Old West gunfighters who had to "take their time in a big hurry." They may literally have dozens of POWs to interrogate. Of course POWs play a deadly game of "hard to find," but it's different from the "witnesses" I pursue—no one has yet tried to shoot me as I approach for information!

INTERROGATIONS INVOLVE MORE THAN JUST ASKING QUESTIONS

My daughter claims that the ability to be a good military interrogator is a gift one is born with—she doubts military interrogation can be learned. She cites as an example a close friend who was also an Arabic linguist who went to every interrogators' school available. "He was not effective because he could not control his temper and was, therefore, a poor actor," she claims.

Military interrogators must be extremely wise, observant, street- and battle-smart people who attain much of their background by looking at and talking to literally hundreds and hundreds of the enemy. Attention to details and subliminal signals must be total. They must also know the culture of the enemy in great detail. Again, using Iraq as an example, Saddam's soldiers were afraid to surrender in spite of the fact that they were desperately hungry, dirty, thirsty, and tired, and many were wounded. Iraqi soldiers were told that everything the Americans ate had pork mixed in. "When they give you a cup of water it probably was the same one used that morning to cook pork!" their officers told them over and over. Coalition forces put the lie to that propaganda by first offering Iraqi POWs oranges and then sealed bottles of water from Saudi Arabia with the labels in Arabic.

We know from TV that Iraqi forces surrendered by the tens of thousands—wave upon wave of them. One bunch, readers will recall, surrendered to an Italian TV crew. My daughter was instructed to be alert for regional dialects among Iraqi soldiers. Some northern dialects suggested to interrogators that these people were not particularly loyal to Saddam. But the war moved so rapidly that interrogation in any form was never a factor.

Skilled military interrogators always want to talk to the people who were present when the prisoner was apprehended to get answers to such questions as: Did he fight bitterly to the end? Were there fellow soldiers who held out along with him? Was his equipment in good shape? What about clothing? Were there designation patches or signs of his rank, unit, or MOS? Were his boots new or used? What about socks? Were such issued? Was he a farm boy who

These people look like civilians, but they're not. They are soldiers who traded their uniforms for civilian clothes and were rounded up for interrogation.

didn't know how to wear boots and socks? Were the shirt and pants new, indicating recent issue? Did they give evidence of being part of a special unit issue? Was the enemy sweeping the bottom of the barrel for supplies in desperation? (An uncle who served in the South Pacific told me they could always determine when they overran a Japanese command company by the presence of peculiar types of small arms carried by the staff soldiers. When that happened, they knew the end of that particular island campaign was in sight.) Was he well fed, or did he look like he was starving? Was he clean and washed? If not, is this really unusual for soldiers from that area and culture? (South Korean infantry, for instance, customarily sleep and live in their foxholes. If they don't look a bit dirty and disheveled, something is going on.) What about medical treatment? Did it appear adequate and effective based on the health of the prisoner?)

When dealing with children my daughter often uses eye movements and body language to evaluate the honesty of their answers. Among the tykes she has the reputation of being impossible to bamboozle. In a military context, she is uncertain whether reading body movements will work. It's too cultural and requires too much interplay with individual POWs, she says. "We usually don't have that kind of time."

INTELLIGENCE GLEANED FROM WEAPONS

Sometimes weapons brought in with prisoners tell a tale, sometimes not. Russian equipment tends to be very generic, carrying few meaningful marks. However, by analyzing the wood in the stocks, the manufacturing techniques exhibited, and the types of magazines on some firearms, it is possible to determine if they are of Chinese, Romanian, or Russian origin. But this information may have little tactical value, just as establishing that an American soldier's World War II Garand was made by Springfield Armory, International Harvester, or Winchester would add little to an enemy's useful intelligence.

Retired Capt. Robin Miller, an army aviator who lost 11 helicopters during his three tours in Vietnam, provides a good example of how intelligence can be gleaned from confiscated weapons. "Midway into my second tour in 1964," he says, "we stopped picking up handmade .45 pistol copies, crude homemade submachine guns, old rusty Japanese rifles, and other battlefield junk pickups. Instead, we were seeing brand-new AK-47s, SKSs, and Makarov pistols. We were also being fired on by 12.7 DShK heavy machine guns by crews with plenty of ammo. Didn't take sophisticated field intelligence to figure out the war had taken a new turn and that lots of additional equipment was coming down the Ho Chi Minh Trail."

Sometimes information recovered from weapons can be misread by those anxious to see something they already believe to be true. Any investigator can fall into the trap of seeing what he wants to see, but this is especially destructive for military interrogators. For example, during World War II ultra-modernistic German MP-44 assault rifles started showing up on the battlefield. U.S. and British intelligence officers looking at the diminutive 8mm steel-cased round and the stamped-steel gun parts assumed this was a last-ditch subsistence manufacturing technique that signaled the end of German manufacturing ability. In fact, it was a dramatically futuristic design, providing significant advantage to German infantrymen.

As you can see, those who interrogate POWs must practically become infatuated with the uniforms, small arms, and equipment they are likely to encounter. When military interrogators are good at their jobs, it won't really matter that much if they can get their captives to talk or not.

Military field interrogators are often confronted by feast or famine. At times they complain about too many bodies to process properly and at other times too few to understand what's really going on "out there." As with domestic spooks, military people must have a "good understanding of the case" before talking to POWs, and they must have a workable plan of action.

MILITARY USE OF PRETEXTS

Do military interrogators also use pretexts? You bet your sweet bippy they do. Hundreds and hundreds of them.

- "I am the top commander in this area, and I am ordering you to tell me the last time you had a hot meal."
- "Now we need to get you to a place of safety so you can quickly return to your family. Tell me quickly how many ranging rounds you fired in your artillery so you can get some warm clothes, food, and water."
- "They let you down by giving you poor, unreliable, dangerous equipment, not resupplying you, and then withdrawing, leaving you to be the sacrificial lamb."

Notice that in the last example the interrogator is giving the prisoner a scapegoat to blame for his present predicament, much like police interrogators and private investigators do.

Of course, being able to come up with viable pretexts

requires that the interrogators have a great interest in and sympathy for the POW's culture and background. As in civilian work, some of these pretexts are pretty wild but must remain eminently credible to the witness.

GETTING PRISONERS TO TALK

My daughter steadfastly maintains that if she can spend a few private moments with each POW away from the crowds, and if she can engage him in some small talk about his units, family, equipment, and circumstances, she can get him to reveal useful information. Muslims (to whom she principally speaks Arabic) believe that nothing they say to a woman is important and are often much more relaxed about talking.

To get a prisoner talking, "ask him about his training," she recommends. That may work if the interrogator knows enough about how the subject to keep up his (or her, in this case) end of the conversation. My daughter spins great, convoluted pretexts based on what the last guy supposedly said or what she supposedly observed from the uniforms and shoes of the other POWs she talked to. Just as in civilian interviews, people start to respond to concern. And when you give them a reason to talk, it's that first bite of peanuts.

There is little said that is of absolutely no value. When lies are obvious, military investigators either confront the liar or ask themselves why this person is spinning this web of intrigue. What does he hope to accomplish? Is he in a position to know the truth? Is his unit so disorganized and dispirited that he believes this weird stuff? How does it all intermesh with the circumstances in which he was captured?

WHO GETS INTERROGATED?

Will key witnesses, such as well-known officers, have enough information to make it desirable to talk to them on several occasions on a number of topics? Perhaps in more of a strategic than a tactical sense, the answer might be yes. Yet, in real life, experts claim that these people (1) are seldom captured unless they wish to be apprehended, (2) fully understand their potential value as POWs as well as the devices that may be used to get them to talk (i.e., they know how and when to keep their mouths shut), and (3) are usually passed quickly "up the line" to people who can work with them more expertly.

All this presupposes that data banks on these key people are available and that we really know whom we have in hand. For example, during the last days of the Third Reich, Allied forces captured a number of Nazis dressed in civilian clothes who were trying to flee Germany. A famous American spy chaser who looked for Martin Bormann for 20 years told me he was fearful about the large number of key Nazis we let slip through our hands because we didn't realize whom we had apprehended. "We just let them go on by," he told me. Many of these escaping Nazis made it to South America and started new lives.

The spy chaser was reasonably understanding, however. "It doesn't happen often that a big fish is caught," he said. "Then it's always toward the end of the conflict when we are overrunning their country, which also happens infrequently these days. Knowing how we got the man, what uniform he wore, whether his name was corroborated by supporting documents, and, most important, where he was taken and with what other people is necessary to determine who we have in custody," he concluded. It is reasonable that front-line soldiers do not realize that the fellow they just passed isn't just another fleeing civilian.

MILITARY INTERROGATORS MUST SPEAK
THE LANGUAGE OF THE PRISONERS

Which brings us to the last question about military interrogations: Can successful military interrogation be done through an interpreter? Most experts believe that the value of responses filtered through an interpreter is limited, especially when visual clues, such as uniforms, insignias, weapons, shoes, and circumstances of the surrender are not available. In some cases when a POW has virtually agreed to switch allegiances, there may be some information of value. But recall the half-life of battlefield information. Experts warn that so much time may have elapsed that any information would be hopelessly stale. Americans do not treat POWs as propaganda opportunities, parading them around like captured animals. Once even an above-average POW is in custody, within 15 days his value is limited.

If a person doesn't speak the language of his prisoner, he should find an interrogator who is fluent in the language, give him the questions he wants answered, and let him go to work. For example, the question might be: "Have they moved the T-72s up to the line?" Ideally, six hours later the interrogator/interpreter will report back: "Looks like they have moved some tanks. I interrogated three people who were probably T-72 crewmen tank mechanics."

"Did they blab a bunch?" the person who requested the information asks.

"No," the interrogator/interpreter responds, "they were pretty cagey and didn't admit anything. I knew they were T-72 people because of their size, their scarred and dirty hands, and the scars on their heads."

Obviously, the interrogator/interpreter knows that T-72 tanks deploy a crew of three, that space in that model tank is extremely limited (necessitating smaller-stature crew members), and that because of limited space and numerous repair problems, heads and hands of crew mechanics often appear beat up He also knows that in that culture hand washing is infrequent. The types of uniforms the prisoners wore and where the prisoners were picked up also provide significant clues.

"So how many tanks have they reinforced with?"

"Let me see if I can determine how many new units are here," the interrogator/interpreter responds.

He may use information from aerial reconnaissance, radio traffic, and bits and pieces of information garnered from other POWs to develop some really outrageous pretexts. Often these pretexts work to secure needed information, but sometimes they don't. Many of the farm boys he deals with don't have a good perspective on what is really happening, anyway.

Anecdotal stories frequently surface about friendly, English-speaking POWs who break down and spill the beans almost immediately, thus causing the entire front to collapse. These tales are usually apocryphal. Farm boys who make up most Third World armies generally do not go to school past sixth grade, so they infrequently learn English! (Plus, average POWs seldom have any concept of the big picture.)

The bottom line is that effective interrogators must speak the language fluently. The U.S. military is committed to that concept, explaining why we go to the trouble and huge expense of sending our soldiers to two years of language training. Although some of us English-only speakers would dearly love to try our hand at military interrogation, unless we go to war with England, we will never have the opportunity!

TIPS ON HOW TO SURVIVE A
MILITARY INTERROGATION

1. Try to leave behind or destroy as much of your uniform and equipment as possible from which clues to your unit, origin, morale, resupply standards, etc., can be deduced.

2. Try to obscure your identity and reason for being there at the time. Come up with a plausible explanation for your presence: "I am part of a veterinarian outfit that just happened to be passing through."

3. Bog down the interrogation with requests for clarification, questions, or trivia. "I don't really understand your English. Could you repeat that please?"

4. Do everything possible to let your command know where you are and, if possible, who you are.

5. Expect to be used for propaganda purposes. Use this opportunity to let people know where you are. Send clever cultural signals if possible.

6. Realize that the longer you can stall, the less valuable any battlefield information you provide will be to your captors.

CONCLUSION

BEING A WITNESS IS TRAUMATIC FOR ALMOST EVERYONE. It's also very interesting. In writing this book it wasn't my intent to upset readers or to give away any professional secrets. I wrote this book for two reasons: to help investigators improve their interview and interrogation skills and to help people who get ensnared in the legal process survive the ordeal. Because of my personal orientation, it was generally written from the perspective of the one doing the interviews. But by knowing how investigators think and act, a witness can learn how to prepare for any interview, deposition, testimony, cross-examination, or interrogation.

Those who want to escape the process completely can obviously use some of this information as well. But I hope that it has become apparent that escaping the long reach of interrogators will not happen unless a tremendous amount of thought, hard work, and diligence are expended.

Why include a section on military interrogations? Readers might be reasonably certain they will not become prisoners of war—but who knows? It is a strange society in which we live, and now readers will know what to expect should they become military or paramilitary prisoners.

As for me, there is a "select" group of people clustered together in one area near where I live who already have become mighty tired of seeing me drive up. At worst, it means one of their friends is in the slammer again; at best, it means that they will now have to spend the next 30 minutes lying, posturing, and telling stories to me! My pretexts for and my effectiveness in dealing with this group of chronic lawbreakers wore thin years ago—as did those of anyone else who's been in the business for long. Great creativity and resourcefulness are required to get any kind of usable information from this class of people.

On the positive side, most of these people are subject to the lure of trading information for cash. The females, especially, tend to feel cut off, abandoned, broke, and without much hope. Cash for information seems to interest them quite a bit, and this is often of great help to me and other investigators.

It should be obvious that all the techniques and pretexts described in this book are clever beyond description, made all the more so by the fact that good investigators (with arguably twisted minds) are thinking about this day and night and learning by trial and error what works and what doesn't. For example, a clever investigator might pose as a pizza deliveryman who happens to take along a small hidden camera with the pizza so he can take photographs of a client's wife who is someplace she shouldn't be, eating pizza with someone she shouldn't be with. Or an investigator might pretend to be a representative of a nonexistent insurance company who is allegedly carrying a large cashier's check payable to A. Disappeared Scuzzball.

Through all of this, keep in mind that in any free, vibrant society nothing happens until a sale is made. After you've read this book, it should be obvious to you that our nation's best salespeople aren't the guys at "Fairly Reliable Bob's Used Chevrolets" or the telemarketers who call at the dinner hour to get you to switch phone services. Likely, the nation's best salesmen are working as private investigators, bringing in information for their clients.

We all know that cops aren't famous for their tact and charm. Dealing with tough, often miserable people all their careers seems to destroy any tact or charm they once may have had. But after reading this book, you should know exactly how to deal with the silver-tongued fox who works part-time nights and weekends for Fairly Reliable Bob's, who is also a police investigator.

Now that even regular citizens who have had little contact with the law know what they are up against, it's time to ask again the question that started this book: Could you resist a determined investigator? Generally, the answer separates the arrogant from the cautious. Recall, we call it "felony stupid" when people think they can BS their way home safe.

Very cautious, very reasoned, intelligent people might stand a chance of avoiding an interview. A friend of mine resolutely maintains that he can resist by saying absolutely nothing. The truth is, he likes to talk and falls for most anything. Odds are, he wouldn't even know he was talking to an investigator rather than signing up for a free trip to Hawaii or some other such pretext.

• • •

Those with questions or comments, please write me in care of Paladin Press (Gunbarrel Tech Center, 7077 Winchester Circle, Boulder, CO 80301 USA). But, please, no letters from private investigators griping about my giving away trade secrets. It really doesn't matter if the rest of the world knows this stuff. They suspect it anyway!